P9-DCB-380

Handy As I Wanna Be

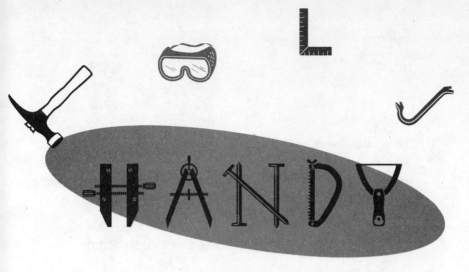

HANDY

AS I WANNA BE

a novel with tools

VINCE RAUSE

POCKET BOOKS

New York   London   Toronto   Sydney   Tokyo   Singapore

POCKET BOOKS, a division of Simon & Schuster Inc.
1230 Avenue of the Americas, New York, NY 10020

Copyright © 1999 by Vince Rause

All rights reserved, including the right to reproduce
this book or portions thereof in any form whatsoever.
For information address Pocket Books, 1230 Avenue
of the Americas, New York, NY 10020

Library of Congress Cataloging-in-Publication Data

Rause, Vince.
    Handy as I wanna be : a novel with tools / Vince Rause.
       p.   cm.
    ISBN 0-671-03284-4
    I. Title.
  PS3568.A826H36   1999
  813'.54—dc21   99-25767

First Pocket Books hardcover printing June 1999

10   9   8   7   6   5   4   3   2   1

POCKET and colophon are registered trademarks of
Simon & Schuster Inc.

Designed by Christine Weathersbee

Printed in the U.S.A.

BP/✖

*To Carmela, Carmela Grace, and Christine,
with all my love*

acknowledgments

Thanks to Randy Rieland of The Discovery Channel Online, who first gave Vinnie a home; to my agent, Arielle Eckstut, for all her hard work and good counsel; to Paolo Pepe for his beautiful jacket design; to Jason Lublinski for his tireless editorial assistance; and to my editor, Emily Heckman, whose guidance was crucial and whose patience in dealing with both Vinnie and me is richly appreciated.

contents

disclaimer

All projects in this book have been carefully tested and approved by me, Vinnie Agita. As far as I can tell, the advice in this book won't get you maimed or brained or anything, unless you do something really stupid, like forget to wear your safety goggles, or fail to follow common sense, or neglect to read your power tool manuals, or lose your patience and maybe try to drive a framing nail with the butt end of a propane torch, which will liven up your life for you, take my word on that one.

Again, I stand behind all the handy wisdom in these pages, but in the interest of fairness I should point out that after years of using noisy, heavy, sharp, and dangerous tools, I am missing several small appendages, am somewhat deaf in my left ear, cannot always remember my middle name, and have so many knots on my head phrenologists give me free readings just for the exercise. On the upside, the doctor says the eyebrows should grow back six weeks tops.

Best wishes,
Vinnie

1
Demolition Man

So I'm out in the yard this morning on a mission from God, breaking up a 550-square-foot concrete slab with a ten-pound sledgehammer, when Angie, my wife, pulls into the driveway. I wish you could have seen me: I was standing on a heap of dusty rubble, all tanned and drenched in glistening sweat. Had my burly work gloves on, my husky steel-toed boots. The battered sledge was resting easily on my shoulder. I must have looked all butch and primal, a regular Stanley Kowalski over here.

From the wide-eyed look on her face, I could see that the whole beefcake, chain-gang package was having a pretty strong effect on the comely Ange, so, to add a little brawny punctuation to the moment, I threw back my head and yelled out "Stellaaa!!! Stellaaaaa!"

Then I swung the hammer overhead and dealt the slab a mighty blow, which chipped off a chunk of rubble about the size of a plum and shot it, like rifle fire, across the yard. Ange didn't even flinch when it shattered the left headlight of her little red Toyota.

Instead, she rolled down the window and asked me in the calmest voice to please put down the hammer. I told her I was just getting warmed up. She nodded and said, "That's fine, Vincent, I can see you've been very busy." I nodded and turned around to show her the work I'd done, but when I turned back again she was furiously backing out of the driveway. Must have forgotten something at the store.

Too bad. I had a few new sledge techniques I wanted to show her. That's right, *techniques.* Sledge work isn't all caveman stuff, Bub. There's a right way and a wrong way.

But before we get to that, let's address the obvious question: Why would anyone this side of an Alabama chain gang take on such a brutal and backbreaking task?

Well, actually, there are lots of good reasons to bone up on your sledge craft: maybe a sewer pipe springs a leak beneath your concrete basement floor or maybe your crumbling, heaving sidewalk is a lawsuit waiting to happen. In either case, some demolition is in order. Sure, you could pay the pros to do the smashing, but plumbers and masons make extravagantly expensive grunt workers. If you do the work yourself you save yourself a bundle. Plus, as you guys know in your hearts, chicks totally dig it.

You might want to rent a jackhammer for larger projects, but in most cases the sledge works fine—concrete, being brittle, shatters more easily than you'd imagine, and in most cases, you'll have the job done and the mess cleaned up in less time than it would take you to make the round-trip to the rental store.

My own concrete-smashing campaign was rather sweeping in scale, so it was taking a little longer. The idea came to me in a vision, while I was fixing some broken crockery in the garage. (Be sure to use lots of fresh airplane glue, and close up all the windows to prevent distracting drafts.)

Things were going smoothly, see, until the word *crockery* popped into my head. I couldn't get over how funny it sounded. I started saying it out loud: Crockery. Crrr-rockery. *Crrr-rocka-rocka-rocka!!*

Anyway, I must have drifted off for a moment because when I came to, the broken pieces of pottery were all glued solid to the workbench, which, at the time, struck me as delightful.

Then, lured by some mysterious impulse, I wobbled over to the garage window to look out upon the blighted little wasteland that passes for our backyard. Like our house itself, the yard had been neglected for decades by previous owners. But while the house retained its innate charm, which lent itself well to my loving renovations, the yard had always seemed beyond reclamation. For starters, it lies on a steep slope, bordered on the uphill side by the high, dingy walls of the house's cinder block foundation. A weather-beaten little balcony, teetering on rusty steel posts, dangles sadly off the kitchen. There's a crumbling stone wall along one property line, and a slender, sorry patch of weedy lawn pitching down into a useless ravine along the other.

As if this charmless little vista was not plug ugly enough, some resident genius decided, maybe twenty years ago, to cover at least two-thirds of the property, and virtually all the backyard's level ground, with a massive slab of concrete. Understand that this is concrete from another age—ragged, hard-core stuff, stained and pitted and studded with horsey pebbles. Over time it had heaved and jutted in crumbling crags like hardened magma that had boiled up from the earth's angry innards to turn my poor little yard into a barren cementatious moonscape.

You just wouldn't want to picnic back there.

It's about eighteen feet wide, this concrete abomination, and it stretches nearly thirty feet from the garage to the house. I can't figure out why anyone would do this to a lawn. Was it someone's idea of a patio? Perhaps they got a bargain on the pour. Or maybe they anticipated a nuclear attack on the neighbor's gazebo and wanted to harden up the property in case any Soviet warheads went off course.

Whatever the motivation, they successfully paved the life out of the yard and left behind a space with all the inviting charm of an abandoned highway under-pass.

The yard had always seemed so discouragingly dreary, in fact, that for the most part, we'd simply ignored it. But this morning, when I stepped to the garage door and gazed out upon it, I was granted a vision. The concrete slab was gone, and in its place was a green, level lawn. That useless slope off to the left had been terraced with handsome herb and veg-etable gardens. Along the back of the house, there was a trim wood deck shaded by a billowy canvas awning and bordered by beds of flowers, and an ivy-covered trellis would screen that ugly foundation wall. Every time I blinked I saw something new: a rose arbor, a picket fence, stout redwood benches that would give this little oasis the cozy ambiance of a green, secluded courtyard.

For a moment, the vision shimmered like a desert mirage, then it got blurry. Then, for an instant, I saw Cindy Crawford dressed like a nun. She pursed her pouty lips suggestively and whispered, "Crockery." Then I got a splitting headache and went over to sit in the shade.

But soon, I understood the meaning of my garden vision. The yard was revealing its potential, telling me how it wanted to be. And as that sunk in, I found myself sputtering in rage at the way my sweet little fraction of an acre had been abused for so long by those who could not understand her. I wanted to set her true spirit free, and to do that, I knew, I had to smash all that evil concrete to smithereens.

So I stepped into the garage, found the sledgehammer, and for the next few hours, plunged into a righteous orgy of vengeful destruction. When I regained my senses, that ugly concrete tonnage had been reduced to a big pile of Kitty Litter. Was it arduous? Indeed. Were there moments of self-doubt? Many. Did the neighbors call the cops when some concrete shrapnel shattered their jug of solar tea? It happens. Still, I labored on, sustained by my glorious vision and my firm grasp of sledgehammer savvy.

What's that? You still don't believe there's craft involved in bludgeoning concrete? Well, I assure you that even in this brutal enterprise, technique is more important than raw strength.

But before we get into that, I've been urged by the skittish legal weasels who run things these days to offer the following disclaimer:

> **Warning.** Swinging a sledgehammer is hard work. You could smash a toe bone. You could get a hernia. You could keel over and croak. So see your doctor before you try this. Get a checkup, a tetanus shot, a brain scan, and a full-body MRI. To be on the safe side, treat yourself to a barium enema or two. Wear eye protection and steel-toed boots and work gloves and a dust mask. Drink lots of fluids. Cut down on fats. Stop smoking. If an eclipse happens while you're

working, do not stare at the sun. Above all, write this message on a piece of paper and tape it to your shirt: "If I am found injured, unconscious, or dead, lying upon a rock pile with a sledgehammer in my hand, I never heard of anyone named Vinnie Agita."

Okay, now let's talk equipment. You'll need an inexpensive sledgehammer to break up the slab, and a pick or long pry bar to loosen up and remove the rubble. You might also want a smaller hammer and crowbar, to dislodge chunks in tight spaces.

One serious note: When you start swinging that sledge, chips will be flying like tracer rounds on Omaha Beach. In the space of a week, my own concrete shrapnel took out the headlight of my wife's car, shattered a garage door window and that jug of solar tea, perforated the back door screen, and, in general, strafed the entire area so furiously that neighborhood cats and squirrels were looking for a U.N. escort out of there.

So naturally, you'll want to take some precautions. Tape cardboard over windows and breakables. Wear loose-fitting long-sleeve shirts and heavy long pants. (If you can lay your hands on some leg guards, like kiddie soccer players wear, you can save yourself from serious abuse to the shinbone.)

Blisters are another curse for sledge swingers, especially on those fleshy pads where the thumb and fingers join the palm, so wrap your hands in Ace bandages, then wear a sturdy pair of work gloves on top.

Above all, wear serious eye protection. Goggles are good, but after taking your first concrete spritz to the mush, you may want to consider a full-face plastic guard. Steel-toed boots can't hurt. And here's a tip: Unless you like the taste of pebbles and portland cement, keep the yapper zipped.

Now let's consider technique. If you want to pound away like some berserk Viking yutz, fine. Just call the nearest emergency room in advance and book some defibrillator time. But I advise you to pace yourself for the long haul.

Let's assume, for example, that you're right-handed. Start with the hammerhead resting on the ground and both hands gripping the base of the handle, right hand over left. Bend your knees and draw the handle toward you with the left hand while the right hand slides up the handle as far as it can go. Then lift with your legs and rotate your torso to smoothly raise the hammer over your right shoulder. Watch your balance . . .

Now, without straining, use your whole body to toss the hammerhead forward so it falls in a natural arc toward the target. Once you get your rhythm down, you can add some ooomph on the downstroke, but for now, concentrate on aim and form. Let the hammer do the work.

When you're finally ready to rumble, take a good balanced stance, aim about four inches in from the edge of the slab, and let the chips fly. Your first few blows may seem discouragingly ineffective, but rest assured you are wreaking havoc on the molecular level.

Soon hairline cracks will appear. Keep pounding, and the cracks will widen into fissures, and then, miraculously, large hunks of rock-hard concrete will crumble under the savagery of your assault.

But be a patient savage. Target one square foot of pavement at a time, looking to break off chunks no bigger that a loaf of bread. When you get one area all nice and crumbly, go in with your pick or pry bar to remove the sundered rubble.

Your pace, of course, will depend upon the thickness and toughness of the concrete you have taken on. Sometimes the stuff shatters like peanut brittle. Other times it becomes a battle for every square inch. But remember, persistence is more important than sheer muscle power. Don't quit. Keep in mind, most of you are smarter than that slab.

For example, today, just as the sun was setting, I encountered a thick section of reinforced concrete that shrugged off my hammer blows like raindrops. It was like pounding on the armored hull of an M1 tank. I must have struck a hundred blows, and all I got were flakes and chips and puffs of powder. But I was driven, and I swung the hammer like a windmill. Sparks flew. I gasped for air. I rained blows like a madman. Finally, with my strength ebbing and my skin going clammy and blue, I mustered one last swing of the hammer, and with a mighty crack, the ornery slab gave up the ghost and shattered into fragments.

A jolt of primal exuberance shot through my veins.

I raised the hammer triumphantly above my head, howled like a timber wolf, and did an Apache victory dance I'd seen on a Bill Moyers special. That's when Ange came back. She had Father Dinucci with her. They brought me a glass of ice water. They made me go sit down.

Father Pete gave me a pastoral smile and said, "I'm just here to help you, Vincent."

I shrugged as I looked him over—the narrow shoulders, the small soft hands—but hey, if he came the whole way over . . .

"I can always use a hand," I said, handing him the hammer, but the weight of the sledge surprised him, and he promptly dropped it on his toe. He yelped some dirty words in Latin as he hopped down the driveway. When he reached his car he turned and made a small but vigorous gesture with a single finger on his right hand. I'd never seen a priest give that particular blessing. But what do I know; I completely lost track of things after Vatican Two.

I shook my head sadly as he drove away. "I've said it for years," I told Angela, "someone ought to come out with a good, sturdy, steel-toed priest shoe." Ange did not respond. Instead, she glared for a fierce nanosecond, then stormed into the house. On another day, I'd have taken this as a sign of anger. But today, something told me that deep down, my hypermasculine sledge frenzy was getting to her, and her display of simmering rage was only the feisty love dance of a passionate and complicated woman. So, with sledge in hand, I followed.

Moments later, I stood in the hallway outside the Agita boudoir, all sweaty and battle scarred, with my leather boots still on, and my sledgehammer at my side. I thumped the floor with the hammerhead stoutly and called out to Ange, "Open the door, honey, it's me . . . Thor."

Angie didn't make a peep. I jiggled the doorknob. The door was locked tight.

"Don't make me take the hinges off," I playfully warned her. Then I heard a series of soft grunts, followed by some scraping and bumping noises, which sounded like our big mahogany armoire being muscled against the door. For a moment, I wondered if I'd misread her signals, but I forced myself to brush away those negative, self-defeating thoughts. To do otherwise simply wouldn't be handy.

2
The Vision Thing

h, the joys of a fresh new handy day. I was up at the crack of dawn, buzzing with how-to zeal. I always get this way when a sexy new project is in the offing. Oh, the plans I had in store for my long-beleaguered backyard! I couldn't wait to share them with Angie, but she'd been acting strange, and I sensed I might need to grease the skids a little. So, when she finally came down to the kitchen, I had a nice big breakfast waiting.

"Beautiful morning," I chirped as I poured her a steaming cup of coffee. She groggily bit into a bagel and acknowledged me only with a sulky groan.

"Sleep well?" I asked.

Ange licked a little strawberry jam from her finger and kept eating, like I wasn't even in the room, then she got up and grabbed a plump ripe peach from a basket hanging over the sink. She was pouting, no question, but I couldn't help noticing that as she walked past the window she gazed, for one wistful moment, at the rubble-strewn backyard.

"Admiring the manly sledge work?" I chuckled.

Ange let out a muffled snicker as she bit into the peach. "Oh yeah, that's some very nice work," she muttered. "You turned the driveway into useless gravel. Now, where are we supposed to park? On the roof?"

Well, I chuckled to myself, *what a ridiculous idea. I mean, parking on the roof would mean decapitating the house, buttressing the rafters with structural steel. You'd have to sink gigantic pylons deep into the earth to support it all, and how in the world would the cars get up there? You'd need a gigantic spiral ramp, like parking garages use . . . unless you had some sort of elevator mechanism. I'd seen them in old carriage houses. They used them to hoist buggies and coaches up through the roof to a second-story garage. True, we'd have to convert the living room into a loading area, but really all you need is a beefy winch and lots of pulleys. . . .*

My reverie was broken by the shock of a half-eaten peach whistling past my ear. "Stop thinking about rooftop parking!" Angie shouted. "Isn't it enough that you destroyed the driveway?"

"I had no choice," I said. "It was handy destiny."

"What are you talking about?" she said.

"Wait here," I said, then I dashed down to my workshop and returned with a rolled-up canvas.

It was a painting, a work of van Gogh–ish intensity done in leftover Dutch Boy enamel, which captured, in bold, impressionistic strokes, my vision of resurrection for our sadly neglected little lawn.

"What's this?" Ange asked sourly.

"It's the future," I said. "It's the backyard as it wants to be. Needs to be. Has every right to be."

As Angie studied the painting, I shared my mystical vision and expressed my passion to do justice to our neglected backyard. "It could be nice back there," I pleaded. "And I promise, I won't do anything without your approval."

Angie tipped her head to the side, noncommittally, playing it cool. But I know this woman. There's a wildness in her. And where there's wildness, you'll find a handy heart, even if it's buried deep.

"Think of it, Ange," I whispered, "a peaceful, secluded backyard retreat. Every time we walked out there, it would be like vacation."

"I don't think I can stand another one of your projects," she muttered, "and this one looks very ambitious."

"We can do it in small stages," I replied.

She shook her head slowly. "I need some details," she said.

I tapped the canvas. "It's all there in the painting," I replied.

Ange nodded absently and pointed at the top left-hand corner of the canvas. "What are these big green pineapples?" she inquired. I checked the painting. "That's topiary," I explained. "Those are human heads. Washington, Lincoln, Jefferson, and Teddy Roosevelt. Mount Rushmore carved out of yew trees!"

Ange gave me a patient frown. "There are five heads here," she said.

"The fifth is Roy Orbison," I explained. "But that's tentative. Five heads might crowd things, and I want to leave room for the Olympic-size boccie court."

"Boccie is not an Olympic sport," said Angie.

"Not yet," I said, "but it's inevitable, and we'll be on the cutting edge!"

Ange smiled wanly as she pulled a fat-tipped laundry pen from a kitchen drawer. She laid the painting on the kitchen table, hunched over it, and started scribbling away. When she handed it back, she had blacked out the yew tree sculptures and written "rose garden" in their place. She had likewise nixed the boccie court, which she had replaced with a small cascading fountain and a water garden. Then my five-story state-of-the-art windmill bit the dust, despite the fact that it would have freed us completely from the tyrannical grip of the greedy power company.

But what really saddened me was her nonnegotiable dismissal of my plan to create a scaled-down diorama of the La Brea tar pits down behind the garage.

"But Ange," I said, "what a conversation piece! T-rexes on the prowl, pterodactyls perched in the trees, a big dim-witted triceratops munching ferns while some sad-sack brontosaurus gets sucked down into the bubbling black slime. . . ."

Angie carefully rolled up the canvas, gripped it like a Louisville Slugger, and smacked me over the head.

"Listen to me," she snapped. "There will be no tar pits, no dinosaur dioramas, no gigantic boccie courts, and no goofy topiary. We will have a nice, normal backyard, like nice, normal people do, or the deal is off."

"Fine," I said. "Then how about a Polynesian theme? I see tiki torches. I see a picnic table made from an over-turned Polynesian war canoe. Maybe I cover the toolshed with palm fronds. Over there, I dredge for a tropical lagoon! And maybe—oh, get this, Ange!—maybe, a working scale model of Krakatoa!"

"Vincent . . . ," muttered Ange.

"It would be a cinch to rig some flashing lights inside the crater."

I was riffing like crazy, but one glance in Angie's direction told me she wasn't sharing the bliss.

"Vincent," she said, calmly, "you need to focus."

"What?" I said.

"Stop riffing. Forget the Polynesian theme."

I shrugged in resignation. "Stick to the basics, is what you're saying."

"I'm saying, no bulldozers, no dynamite, and the minute you try to have anything delivered by helicopter, I will nip your handy urges in the bud, if you catch my drift."

I nodded with a dutiful wince. "Does this mean the project is a go?" I asked her.

"I'll take this to work and think it over," she said as she rolled up the canvas.

"I won't lift a finger without your okay," I said, with the biggest, most amicable smile I could manage.

"On second thought," she said, tapping my chest with the painting, "just don't do anything at all."

3
My Hardware Guy, Phil

It was 3 A.M., and I was pacing at the foot of the bed, thoroughly jazzed with the thrill of a large, looming handiness and waiting eagerly for dawn, when I stubbed my toe on the foot of the four-poster. I tried mightily to stifle my yells of pain, but no luck. I woke up the light-sleeping Ange.

"Get back in bed," she muttered, tugging a pillow over her head.

"Can't sleep, Babe," I answered. "Too excited about the backyard makeover scheme."

Ange grumbled softly beneath the pillow. "See," she said, "this is how you get into trouble. You agitate yourself, you make bad decisions, next thing you know you're blowing up someone's garage, or setting fire to someone's gazebo. . . ."

"I can't help it," I replied as I leapt to my feet. "My head is just bursting with ideas!"

"I know it's important to you," said Angie, "but this is not the time for rash action; this is the time to think, the time to plan, the time to reflect upon goals and tactics."

Yeah, I thought, maybe. Or maybe it's time to rent me a big, snortin' hog of a power washer and scrub about fifty years of grime and crud from the exterior foundation of my house.

A power washer, for those unhandy souls who do not know, is basically an industrial-strength Water Pik on wheels. There's a beefy air compressor with a heavy-duty intake hose attached. Water flows in through the hose and is pumped out the handheld spraying wand with enough turbo-charged velocity to scour barnacles off a battleship. Just the weapon for those crummy foundation walls.

Why power wash my foundation, you ask? Because the successful renovation of my ugly-yet-soon-to-be-charming little yard demands it. I'd already begun that project by smashing our old, oafish concrete driveway to bits. Next will come a sweeping campaign of reclamation: I'll lay new sod, plant new shade trees and shrubbery, put in an herb garden, some rose arbors, a rustic garden bench or two, a canopied flagstone patio, and whatever outdoor grace notes Ange might request.

So the vision was clear, but none of it could happen until I dealt with the harsh reality of that horsey concrete block foundation, which would provide the backdrop for all my planned improvements and which, at present, lent to my little half acre all the charm of the exercise yard at Attica.

Oh, it was ugly, that wall, all pitted and stained and streaked with decades of sooty grime. But I had a plan. First, I'd paint the wall a soft, natural hue, then screen it from view with a row of tall, ivy-bearing trellises. But, as even the greenest handy guy among you understands, a good paint job requires a grit-free, grease-free, soot-free surface. My foundation was none of those. I could have scrubbed the blocks with a wire brush, I guess, but I have better things to do with the next six months of my life. Hence, my dance of destiny with a power washer from hell, which I rented the next morning from my hardware guy, Phil.

Phil runs the Hardware Hut, a dusty little hardware emporium where I take most of my business. Phil's place is dark and cramped and badly in need of a paint job. His selection is meager. His service is rude. His prices are outrageous. But I go there because of Phil's tough-love approach to the handyman–hardware guy relationship. (Well, actually, I go there because it's the only hardware store in town that still lets me roam the aisles without a security escort, but the tough-love thing is important too.)

How does tough love figure into the hardware game? Simple: Like all great hardware guys, Phil knows that as a true handyman I am fire and passion and impulse, and that as the hardware guy, he must provide the wisdom and restraint that give shape to my vision and allow me to recklessly explore all my raw handy urges.

I can't say exactly how he does it, he just has a way, but the moment I walk into that store and bathe in Phil's portly, White Owl–chomping aura, I get all energized and focused. Tough love will do that. Take, for example, the elaborate ritual he performed when he saw me step through the door.

"All right, Agita," he barked as he shoved an empty cardboard box across the counter, "you know the drill."

I nodded in can-do fashion, and emptied my pockets into the box. I tossed in pencils, lip balm, my comb, my keys, my Leonard Cohen Pez dispenser, and a lot of other clutter, including the hollow plastic barrel of a ballpoint pen I keep on hand in case an emergency tracheotomy is ever in order. (I'm defining do-it-yourself very broadly these days.)

When I finished, Phil examined the box, then plucked a plump smooth pebble from the pile.

"What's this?" he asked, gnawing on his stogie.

"It's my pet rock, Iggy," I said. "He's igneous."

Phil just stared, working his tongue to loosen a scrap of tobacco from between his incisors. Then, rousing himself with a gruff snort, he grabbed the box and stashed it under the counter.

"Is that everything?" he asked.

"I'm clean," I said, turning my pants pockets inside out.

"No sharp implements?"

"Nope."

"Any small explosive charges?"

"Negatory," I said, drumming on the counter for emphasis.

"Any biological wastes or toxic liquids?"

"That's just my Hai Karate," I explained.

Phil grunted in satisfaction. "Now," he said, "let me hear you recite the rules."

I clicked my heels and snapped to attention. "Rule number one," I said, "all sales final."

"Yup," said Phil.

"Rule number two: I broke it, I bought it."

"Bingo."

"And rule number three: stay way the hell out of the flammable solvents section."

"Good," said Phil. "Now, what do you need?"

I wheeled to face the rental section and pointed at the biggest, baddest pressure washer in the store. "I want that," I said.

"The Tsunami Two Thousand?" cried Phil. "Forget about it."

"What?" I whined in protest.

Phil jabbed his cigar in the Tsunami's general direction. "That's an industrial-caliber machine," he said. "Shoots a stream of water so powerful, it'll carve stone. Sending you home with that monster would be like handing a lunatic a surgical laser."

"I can handle the machine," I grumbled.

"It's out of the question," said Phil. "It's a matter of public safety. I couldn't live with myself if anyone got hurt."

"I'll pay you double," I offered.

"Triple," said Phil, "and you pay for the gas."

Once money had changed hands, Phil wheeled the Tsunami up to the checkout desk, then he slapped a thick book on the counter.

"Read this," said Phil.

I looked at the cover. "Oh, come on," I said, "this is the safety manual. What kind of baby reads the safety manual?"

"You want the machine or not?" Phil barked.

"But I'm a seasoned handyman. . . ."

"Your track record isn't good," Phil muttered. "Need I mention the self-propelled rototiller I rented you last summer? I told you not to leave the engine running."

Oh, that. Damn machine gave me the slip when I went in the house for a brewski. Didn't even notice it was missing for twenty minutes, and by then it had already chewed its way through several neighboring gardens to emerge down at the corner park where, apparently, it made some threatening advances against joggers and geese, so the cops had to shoot it.

"Freak accident, Phil," I said. "Must have been solar flares or something."

Phil tapped the safety manual. "Read it. Now," he said.

Exasperated, I grabbed the manual and plopped in a nearby folding chair. "Okay, let's see what we got," I said as I flipped open the pages. "Says here: Number one—Do not power wash infants; number two—Do not attempt to clean nozzle with tongue while power washer is in operation; number three—Power washer is not licensed for the practice of colonics."

"All right, gimme that," growled Phil. "If you're going to be a wise guy, no power washer for you."

"Lighten up, Phil," I said, chuckling. "Give me the damn book." For the rest of the afternoon, I plowed through a few hundred pages of uptight blather about the importance of properly operating the Tsunami. The gist could be boiled down to this: Screw around, and you could blind yourself, or lose a hand, or blast all the hair off your head, and similar warnings of gloom and doom.

(Don't these control freaks make you nuts with their constant doomsday whining: Don't smoke in bed, don't go swimming after a heavy meal. Know what I like to do just to cheese them off? I wait for a total eclipse of the sun, I go outside, I stare right the hell at it. Day and a half, tops, your sight comes back and you have the last laugh.)

When I was finished reading I handed the manual to Phil.

"Okay, boss," I said, "I get the picture—this is one mean machine."

"You better believe it," Phil replied, "and you better

listen to what I'm saying now. The Tsunami comes with five different nozzles. See these numbers stamped into the brass? Each nozzle is numbered I through V. Don't go higher than nozzle II. Nozzle III and higher are for military purposes only."

I promised Phil I'd tow the line, then I rolled the Tsunami out the door.

It took just a few minutes to connect the big machine to an outdoor faucet and gas up the tank. All that remained was to choose a nozzle, and go to town. I promised Phil I'd stick with nozzle II, but when I saw nozzle V sitting there so bright and sparkly, I figured, what the hell, let's see what she can do.

So I snapped number V onto the tip of the spray wand, gave the starter cord a tug, and felt the Tsunami surge alarmingly to life. As I felt the supply hose throb with vigor I knew this was all the machine I had hoped for and more. So powerful was the spray, in fact, that I could barely control the spray wand. It wanted to go all silly. I tried hard to keep a steady aim at the wall, but the Tsunami writhed in my hands like a python, and the stream moved in big loops across the foundation. In amazement, I realized that the laserlike spray was actually carving a groove into the concrete blocks. I mean, I could have written my name with it.

And that was no good at all, so I jiggled the trigger to toggle off the on lock, but the lock would not release. I couldn't shut off the spray, so I instinctively aimed the wand skyward, only to shear the overhead power lines like a hot knife cutting through linguini. Now the cables dangled on the ground all around me, sparking and spitting and sizzling as they danced like snakes. I had to get out of there so, in a panic, I jammed the nozzle of the power washer's wand into the lawn between my feet, hoping to stifle the spray. Instead, the earth exploded into a swirling funnel cloud of soggy turf and tiny bits of grass, which plastered me head to toe with a slimy coating of mossy green. I looked like a freshly watered Chia Pet.

Then my foot tangled in the water hose, and down I went, and as I tumbled the alarmingly potent water spray cut a random path of destruction, which seemed to pass in superslow motion: a row of roses was beheaded, our new brass yard lamp exploded into bits, the neighbor's electric blue lawn ball was shattered, then the wand swung down and the laserlike stream neatly sheared off both rubber-coated toes of my new canvas sneakers.

Finally, I worked my way to the spigot and was able to shut off the water and bring the soggy mayhem to a close. The experience humbled me, though, so when things settled down I replaced nozzle V with nozzle I, which, as it turned out, had all the power I needed to quickly chase the grime from my basement walls.

Immediately, I realized what a useful tool this power washer could be. It not only scoured the foundation blocks crisply clean, but it also chased old grime and algae stains off the sidewalks and dramatically freshened up the red brick walls of the house. I used it to blast hardened grass clippings from the underbelly of my lawn mower and to scour the baked-on crud from a neglected gas grill. I gave all my muddy garden tools a generous, cleansing spritz, then I lent the machine to my neighbor, who turned it loose on his graying, weather-beaten deck and watched as the hard-working spray brought back the tired wood's old brightness and color.

Meanwhile, when the foundation was dry, I patched up gaps and gouges with mortar, then sealed the walls with a coat of a good oil-based primer, using a stiff-bristled brush to work the primer into the rough, pitted surface of the block.

Then I rushed the power washer back to the Hardware Hut and raced home again to begin my furious campaign of damage control. A quick call to the electric company got the power lines fixed (when they started asking questions I mumbled something about secret air force tests and low-flying planes). Then, it was just a matter of fixing what I could, and disguising the rest of the damage.

I had just finished installing the new yard lamp when Angie got home. She was impressed by the progress I'd made, and I told her that after the primer was dry, I'd brush on several coats of exterior enamel. I told her she could pick the color.

We went inside, where the beheaded roses were waiting for her in a crystal vase. I made dinner, we drank some wine, I excused myself to slip into the Matt Helm robe and shiny faux-gator slippers, and when I returned all signs pointed toward an evening of Love, Agita Style. . . .

So I got out the concertina and started playing "Return to Sorrento," making the chords tremble romantically, which always gets to Ange, and predictably, she got all limp and dreamy.

Then I wiggled my tootsies from my slippers, the better to play footsies with. "O Angie," I sighed, "your eyes, your lips, your hair—"

"Vinnie," said Ange, "your little toe."

Well, I thought, here's a new direction.

"No," said Ange. "Your little toe . . . where is it?"

I glanced down at my foot. Sure enough, my little toe had been neatly severed at the second joint.

"Wow," I whispered in handy awe, "no blood, no pain. That really was an amazing machine."

4
Mrs. Plumpton's Gnomes

dded a new tool to my arsenal this week—an industrial-quality, pneumatically powered nail gun, which relates to the conventional framing hammer, ordinance-wise, as an AK-47 relates to your basic mallet.

Pow! Pow! Pow! This baby nails with the ease of thought. It's just what I need to make that backyard project go swiftly and smoothly. I'll knock off the deck in no time. Building the arbors and benches will be a breeze. No calluses. No finger fatigue. Just the soft pop of nail after nail after nail being shot home straight, and deep, and true.

A great tool. Worth every penny. If only it fired a little *faster.* That's what I spent my money for, speed, and when I tried it out the other day, it seemed just the teensiest bit sluggish. So I opened up the gun housing and fiddled with the firing mechanism just a smidgen, looking for ways to goose the gun's gusto.

While I was working, I heard a truck idling in the street, and when I peeked out the window, I couldn't believe my eyes. It was a van from Muhlenhorst's Nursery and Garden Supply, delivering more plaster garden gnomes to old Mrs. Plumpton next door.

I hustled out to the sidewalk. Old lady P. was directing the workmen from her porch as they carried the gnomes off the van.

"Hi, Mrs. P.," I called out. "More gnomes?"

"Stay on your property," she screeched.

"Quite a few gnomes back there already," I cried. "Plenty of gnomes in the yard." Last count, I'd tallied forty-seven.

"Free country!" she barked. "Go away!"

I bristled as I watched the gnomes being set in their places, a whole new brigade of little gremlins with evil elfish grins. Oh, their nasty little pointy beards, their gnarled little hands. Clutching miniature lanterns. Wielding tiny picks. Playing their devilish little fiddles.

"Look," I said, "there are ordinances about things like this. Just so many gnomes to a yard!"

Mrs. Plumpton glared at me, "Gnome-hater!" she cried. "Elf-bigot! You leave my little friends alone!"

Then she rushed into the house and slammed the door behind her.

When Ange got home from work, I told her about the new shipment of trolls.

"Gnomes," she said, "not trolls."

"What?" I said. "You're on her side?"

"You're being silly," she replied. "She's just an old lady."

"Doesn't it worry you, the things she does with them?" I said. "Remember? Last Easter? The Last Supper gnome tableau?"

"I didn't think that was so bad," said Ange. "But I really like what she did for Kwanza."

I smacked my head. "She's a lunatic, Ange."

"She's eccentric," Ange replied. "Those gnomes are like pets to her. She even has names for them."

"I do too," I answered. "Sleepy. Dopey. Grumpy. David Berkowitz. Travis Bickel . . ."

Angie patted me on the shoulder. "You have to get over it, Vinnie," she said laughing. "They're just little plaster statues."

"They're evil, Ange," I snarled. "Look in their eyes. They hate."

I couldn't sleep that night—I kept having nightmares about a ten-foot-tall Billy Barty—so around midnight I went down to the kitchen for a snack. As I passed the dining room window, I peeped through the miniblinds out into the darkness, and down on Mrs. Plumpton's gnome-infested yard. Something seemed odd down there, and when I flipped on the outdoor floodlights, my neck hairs stiffened like wire. All the gnomes—there must have been sixty by now—were turned to face my house! They were smiling their diabolical smiles, sucking on their little corncob pipes, playing their miniature accordions and tambourines!

The horror!

I killed all the lights and stood watch by the window all night. Each time I looked out, I could swear the gnomes had inched closer. I kept up the vigil until just before dawn. Angie found me asleep on the floor in the morning, but she wasn't buying into my living nightmare.

"You imagined it," she said as she hoisted up the blinds. "See for yourself." I looked down into sun-drenched Gnomeland. All the little plaster weasels were back in their usual spots.

"I'm telling you, Ange, it was horrifying," I said. "She's gaslighting me, and that's not neighborly."

"Look," she said, "I'm late for work. But I'm going to say this one last time: No more Hostess Sno Balls binges before bedtime."

So I showered and shaved and tried to push Mrs. Plumpton's gnomes from my mind. After all, it was a beautiful day, with wide handy horizons.

Specifically, it was time to test my new souped-up nail gun. I hoped the modifications I'd made would more than double the nail-per-second firing rate, but there was only one way to find out. So I leaned some old two-by-twelve planks against the front of the garage, cranked up the compressor, and prepared to rock and roll.

"Be careful with that thing, you idiot!" cried Mrs. Plumpton. "You're going to kill somebody!"

I reassuringly held the gun up in the air. "No need to worry," I said. "This baby has a special safety, built right in. It won't fire unless the muzzle is pressed tight against a piece of wood. Watch," I said. "Even if I press the trigger—"

Now, I could make up a lot of excuses here, but that's just not my style. The truth is, my misguided modifications had not only disabled the nail gun's safety, they had also turned the power nailer into a fire-breathing tool of death. Nails no longer "fired" from the muzzle, now they *streamed,* they *gushed.* To make matters worse, the trigger jammed in the firing position, and as I struggled to free it, my feet tangled in the air hose running to the compressor, and as I tumbled across the lawn, chevrons of big pointy galvanized framing nails zipped through neighboring yards like swarms of angry, deadly bees.

It's funny, the things you remember. I can see leaves being nipped off the Finsterwalds' mulberry tree. I recall the crash, the sparks, and the sizzle as the Pointdexters' bug zapper shattered to pieces and gave up the ghost.

The rest was a blur until Ange filled me in after the officers left.

"They found some old lady's pillbox hat nailed to a telephone pole out front," she muttered.

"But no old lady?" I asked, in a hush.

"They found her cowering in the Tuppertons' shrubbery."

I sighed in relief. "Well, look on the bright side, Ange: At least there weren't any casualties."

"Tell that to the Hammermyers' potbellied pig," Angie replied. "He's at the vet, thrashing and squealing. They think it's post-traumatic stress."

That made me sad. "I'll buy the pig some apples," I said.

"Good start," said Ange, "but you're also going to have to rebuild his little pig house, including the pink gingerbread trim and the toy satellite dish on the roof."

"Done." I eagerly complied.

"And what about the Peabodys' above-ground pool?" she said. "You turned that into a gigantic lawn sprinkler."

"Nothing a gross or two of inner-tube patches can't fix."

"And then there's Mrs. Plumpton's gnomes," she said. "You shot them up like so many plaster skeet."

I waved off the comment. "She has so many gnomes," I grumbled. "She won't even notice."

"She noticed," said Ange. "She talked to the cops. They say you had motive—"

"It was an accident!" I insisted.

"She agrees not to press charges," said Ange, "if you agree to fix the gnomes. Mostly, you shot off noses and fingers and little pointy beards. She gave me a list of the injured. Looks like Gnome Chomsky lost most of his butt. And you blasted the little toy pitching wedge right out of Greg Gnome-an's hands."

I stared blankly.

"What?" said Ange.

I crossed my arms. "I don't do gnomes," I muttered.

"You don't do gnomes?"

"I'm no gnome jockey," I said. "I'm not touching those stumpy little cretins."

Ange sat next to me on the couch and pressed my hands between her palms.

"Let me tell you something, Vinnie," she said, softly. "You're going to fix all those gnomes. Every single one of them. Until you do, you are grounded in all things handy. You get me? No projects. No tools. I don't even want you changing a light bulb."

"But what about the backyard project?" I begged. "You promised."

"Forget the backyard," Angie snapped.

"You can't make me give up the dream," I pleaded.

Ange stood up and gave me a nonnegotiable glare. "Your handy life is over, Bub, until those gnomes are whole again."

When she gets like that, it's no use talking, and I know when I am beat. So I found a big canvas tarp in the basement, dragged it over to Mrs. Plumpton's yard, and began the mournful, dreadful work of gathering up the shattered gnomes. When I got them back home, I converted my workshop into a field hospital, laid out all the broken parts, and began the grisly process of triage. Moments later, Ange came down the basement stairs. She staggered at the bottom, pretending to swoon over the carnage around her.

"It's not funny, Ange," I snapped. "I'm going to have nightmares about this for the rest of my life."

5
Raging Bull

The next morning I got up early and had a tasty continental breakfast waiting for Ange as she stumbled down the stairs. Fresh-squeezed orange juice. Bagels and sweet rolls. Honeydew melon. A big pot of French-roast java. If the gesture cut any ice, Angie's groggy silence didn't show it. I decided to proceed as if nothing was wrong.

"Raining again," I said.

She bit into a bagel and acknowledged me only with a sulky mumble.

"This weather's wreaking havoc with my backyard plan," I said. "And it's been quite a while since I've done anything handy."

Ange licked a little raspberry jam from her finger, like I wasn't even in the room.

"Anyway," I continued, "I know we made a deal that I wouldn't start any new projects until the backyard is done, but with the rain and all, I'm getting a little antsy, and I was thinking, maybe I could do some little fix-up job around the house. Something minor. Just to vent a little handy-steam."

Ignoring me, Angie used the nail of her little finger to delicately wiggle a morsel of bagel free from her teeth.

"For example," I said, "how about I rip out the leaky old toilet in the powder room and replace it with one of these new siphon-jet, space-age beauties? They're doing some wonderful things with flush technology these days."

Ange looked right through me.

"Or," I suggested, "I could get one of those do-it-yourself sauna kits and build a little Scandinavian spa out in the garage."

Ange yawned and downed her orange juice like a shot of Canadian Club.

"Here's another thing: I was smelling a rankness in the basement all night," I told her. "Could be a break in a sewer line. Might not be a bad idea to rent an air hammer, break up some of the concrete slab, and do some exploratory surgery. . . ."

Angie lowered her coffee cup and shot me a chilling glare. "Are you talking to me?" she grumbled, like a young De Niro in hair rollers and fuzzy slippers. Reconnoitering, I cocked my head sideways and smiled. "Hey," I said, "have you lost weight?"

Ange snorted in exasperation and went up to get ready for work. When she came down again I had a fresh cup of coffee waiting.

"Ange," I said, "I'm so bored. Please let me fix something."

"Fix the gnomes," she said.

I shrugged, and rocked on my heels.

"What?" said Ange, stuffing her keys into her purse.

"I can't," I admitted. "I'm afraid to be around them when I'm home alone."

Ange muttered under her breath as she swept up her briefcase and headed for the door, but she stumbled on a throw rug, and as she whirled to keep her balance, the point of her narrow-tipped heel gouged a small, deep divot into the floor.

"Oh . . . look at that gouge," I whispered, feeling light-headed and oddly aroused.

Ange shrugged. "These old floors are already shot," she said. "We should lay down wall-to-wall."

"But Angie, it's virgin oak," I said.

"Some virgin," she replied. "Look at all the dents and scratches. It's like the Lord of the Dance was here, in golf shoes."

Then she shot me a warning scowl, for general purposes, and disappeared out the door.

I looked around the room. Ange was right, the floors were a disaster. I told myself, Ange deserves much better. She shouldn't have to put up with floors like these. And while she may be thinking she doesn't want to endure the noise, or the mess, or the many possible mishaps of allowing me to sand and refinish the floors, how could she know what she wants until she sees how beautiful this old wood could be with just a little caring handy attention?

In retrospect, I had no choice. So I emptied the rooms, raced off to the Rental Ranch, and returned an hour later with a big beefy bull of a floor sander—one hard-boiled piece of hardware if ever there was one. All bulbous steel and raw horsepower and sneering industrial-strength *attytood*. Parked by the mantel, it looked menacing and satisfyingly macho, like what you might get if you let those Low-Rider kids down the block soup up your Hoover.

Anyway, I couldn't wait to get started, so I plugged in the heavy-duty power cord, gripped the nubbly rubber handles, fired up the engines, and started to rock and roll.

Instantly, the floorboards trembled beneath my feet as the sander's motor sang out in a robust, throaty growl—it was the song of merciless, grinding conquest. I let the rotation of the sanding belt tug the machine steadily forward, and watched as it chewed its way across the dull, battered floor, spewing ruddy dust and leaving a fresh swath of pale golden oak in its wake.

So moved was I by the beauty of this handy moment that I threw my head back and howled like a timber wolf. In retrospect, this may not have been prudent, since in my moment of distraction the sander gave me the slip and took off, like a bull on the streets of Pamplona, after Angie's octogenarian Aunt Lucretia, who, without knocking, had absentmindedly bumbled, all stooped and bowlegged and wobbly, into the house and straight to the heart of Handy Ground Zero.

"Lucretia!" I shouted. "Veer left!"

For a moment, the poor old babe froze like a deer in the glow of the sander's halogen headlight, but at the last second she gathered her wits and dodged the sander's charge, showing a flash of the lightning-quick foot speed that had earned her the silver medal in the singles freestyle competition at the Greater Palermo Chianti Stomp-Off of 1937 (long program).

Still, Lucretia was not out of danger, as the sander had bounced off the baseboard and once again drawn a bead on her ample old-world keister. Her black lace shawl streamed behind her as she made a frantic bolt for the doorway, but the sander was closing fast.

"Zig left!" I called to her as the big machine roared forward. "Zig right!" All the while, I was positioning myself for a rescue, and when I saw my chance I lunged toward her and pushed Lucretia out of harm's way. Then the big machine came at me, but at the last second I pirouetted from its path with the grace of a matador (though matadors do not generally warble "woob-woob-woob" like Curly the Stooge) as the sander rumbled into the corner and smashed against the wall, where it grumbled and fidgeted like a wild pig rooting for truffles. By the time I pulled the plug, it had chewed out a neat little bowl-shaped trough in the floor.

"Dust in the afternoon," I whispered in tribute as the good brave sander quivered and fell silent.

I could have brooded over that oaken divot for a long time, but behind me, I felt the gathering power of what my highly attuned Mediterranean senses told me was an imminent thunderclap of bottomless Sicilian rage, radiating from the very corner into which my life-saving intervention had sent Lucretia flying, all a-tumble.

"Eyyyyyy 'andy-Mahhhhn!" she muttered in a soft, venomous hiss. "I give-a you 'andyman."

When I turned around she was still dusting herself off. But I knew she was going to curse me. I've seen it all before. First she hitches up her black apron as she conjures up some Old Country mojo. Then she hunches forward like a wrinkly welterweight and commences this ooga-booga wiggly eye thing followed by some furious foot shuffling, which for some reason I find particularly alarming. (Must be the scrabbling of those nasty old black orthopedic nun's shoes she's fond of wearing.)

The curse itself is delivered by flicking the thumbnail sharply against the dentures. To be on the safe side, I always just lam it out of range and head for the nearest large quantity of holy water, which in our neighborhood, can be found most readily in the sanctuary of the parish church—Our Lady of Constant Reeling Sorrows.

As I bolted out the door, I knew Lucretia had no chance to keep up with me, since I know all the backyard shortcuts. (Though she was gaining on me until I lost her for good in the Finsters' backyard when her hair net got snagged on a low-hanging branch.)

Out of danger, I backtracked to my car, grabbed the empty gas can from the trunk, and headed, in a loping jog, toward the church. As I made my way I reflected on my complex relationship with Angie's only great-aunt. It goes way back to the days when Ange was single. Lucretia wanted Ange to marry Tony Pantalone, not only because his name rhymes nicely, but also because his family has a thriving wholesale produce business. To Auntie L, who grew up under the constant threat of famine, produce means survival.

"You marry Tony," she would say to Angie, "and even if he turns out to be a stinky bum, hey, you still gonna have a nice salad."

But Ange married me instead, and ever since, Aunt Lu-Lu's been raining down her magical fury upon me. One time she visited a really bad sock wedgie on me when we were driving cross-country; another I got a really wobbly table every time we went out to eat for three months running. (Once, she even made the drawstring of my sweatpants disappear maddeningly inside the waistband, and I had Jazzercise that night.)

Moments later I bounded into the church, where I found Father Pete tidying up the altar. "Fill 'er up!" I called down the aisle as I banged on the gas can. "Not another curse," said the Padre, with a stern clerical scowl.

"I think she nailed me this time," I explained.

"I'm not giving you a gallon of holy water," he carped. "There's a drought on, you know."

"Then maybe some blessed oil?" I cajoled. "Some leftover Lenten ashes? Maybe a quick preventative exorcism—you can do that on an outpatient basis, right?"

Father Dinucci gave me a long, studious stare, like I'd just grown a third eye. Then he smiled officiously. "Your faith is admirable," he replied, "but none of that stuff is really certified for curses."

"But, Father," I implored, "you have to give me something."

The good father drew a deep breath and rolled his eyes to the ceiling. "Try this," he said. "Make a little beanie out of tin foil, and wear it all the time."

"Is that Vatican approved?" I asked. It sounded a little heretical to me.

"It's an experimental program," he said, as he patted me kindly on the shoulder. "For individuals of a certain ilk, it seems to provide relief."

I knew that Lucretia had already filled Ange in concerning our unfortunate sander mishap, so when I got home I set about making the basement a little homier, since I didn't need Alvin Toffler to predict that I'd be sleeping down there for a while.

So I hauled in a battered old BarcaLounger from the garage, hung up my pictures of dogs playing poker, and rigged up a bootleg cable connection for my portable TV. And since I knew the main living areas of the house, including the kitchen, would be off limits while Ange was home, I gathered up a cache of the salty, greasy snacks without which no evening's relaxation is complete. I stashed the junk food behind the water heater, made myself comfortable, and waited for Ange to come home.

When finally I heard her footsteps coming down the basement stairs, I braced myself for a memorable Sicilian tongue-lashing. Instead, she just nodded hello and handed me a sheet of paper.

"What's this?" I asked.

"It's an affidavit stating that you will cease and desist all handy activity from this day forward," she said, "until such a time as you have proven, to my satisfaction, that you have gained control of freaking handy lunacy before you kill somebody."

I read the document over. "It says here no handy projects whatsoever," I pointed out.

"That's right," she answered. "Zilch. Zero."

"Except for the yard, you mean," I said. "It's supposed to be sunny tomorrow."

"Including the yard," said Ange.

"But it was Lucretia's fault," I grumbled. "She lumbered right into the line of fire. And I risked my life to save her."

VINCE RAUSE

"It's always someone else's fault," said Ange, with a tone of patience and sympathy in her voice that really made me jumpy. "The problem lies within. But don't worry, we're going to beat this thing together."

Then she kissed me lightly on the forehead, climbed the stairs, and closed the basement door upon me.

I passed the evening quietly. I watched a little bowling on TV. Read the sports page. Did some Callanetics.

At nine o'clock, I felt like a snack, so I gathered up my treats, settled in the recliner, and tuned in *Mannix* reruns on channel sixty-four.

Then I tore into the munchies. First, I devoured ranch-flavored pork rinds, licking the iridescent orange residue from my fingers when I was through. Then I gobbled a fistful of honey-roasted peanuts and a bowlful of greasy Pizzarinos. And when my thirst was raging and my tongue was coated by a thick biochemical goo, I pulled a precious frosty brewski from a cooler I kept under the stairs. The can felt slick and heavy in my hand. I savored, in anticipation, the first long, quenching gulp. But when I tugged at the pop-top, the aluminum ring snapped off uselessly in my fingers, rendering my golden suds utterly unattainable.

Not to worry, since I'd also stashed a backup brew. But forces beyond my control seemed to be in action now, and horror consumed me as, once again, the pop-top opener failed. There would be no quenching flow to silence my raging thirst.

"Damned Sicilian devil woman," I whimpered, as I fell back in torment upon my lumpy sofa. In the darkness I could hear the distant tinny cackle of Lucretia's taunting laughter, unless it was just my Reynolds Wrap beanie crinkling against the cushions.

6
Ohmm Sweet Ohmm

ne week later I stood at the bedroom window, watching glumly as a late-afternoon cloudburst unleashed its watery fury and turned my little backyard into a sodden bog of broken dreams.

"Another washout," said Angie, patting me gently on the back.

"The backyard's a quagmire," I said. "It's been raining all week. I'll never get to work on my backyard project. Damn El Niño."

"The sun will come out soon," Angie replied as she headed for the master bath.

"It's been so long since I did anything handy," I said, sighing.

"Fix the gnomes," she mumbled as she buttered up her toothbrush and scrubbed at her incisors.

Inwardly, I cringed. "I'd love to," I lied, "but I had to order a special high-tech gnome adhesive, and I can't start until it arrives."

Ange pulled the toothbrush from her mouth and shot me a warning scowl. "Remember our deal," she said. "No new handy projects until the backyard is finished."

"But, Ange," I protested, gesturing toward the rain.

"A deal is a deal," she said. "No new handy projects. Now get dressed, I don't want to be late for the party."

Ange was dragging me to the grand opening of a local New Age bookshop—Ohmm Sweet Ohmm, it's called—which is run by her cousin Gina. She didn't come out and say it, but I think she was hoping I'd find some inner peace, and maybe a less disruptive hobby, there among all the crystals and the incense and the spiritual wisdom of the ages. Being scandalously unhip to the New Age scene—except for that beefy phone bill I've run up with the Psychic Friends Network—I wasn't sure what I was getting into, so I sulked the whole time we were in the car.

But I have to admit, when we walked into the store, I dug the place from the get-go. They had scented candles burning. There was spooky outer space music floating in the air. People were gathered in hushed groups, channeling over here, Rolfing over there. I found it placidly intoxicating. And as I adjusted to the energy of the place, I felt a primal vibration rumble deep inside me, which could have been my soul resonating in concert with the rhythms of the universe, unless it was that double-cheese gardenburger and fries I stopped for on the way over.

We were met in the doorway by a young man wearing a blousey white shirt with a drawstring at the collar, like something a sixteenth-century French fencing master might wear. According to his nameplate, his name was Dustin, and his title was assistant manager/shaman trainee.

"Welcome to Ohm Sweet Ohm," he said as he waved a scrawny twig in our faces. "This is a holly branch, which, according to many traditions, has the power to cleanse the mind and ease the spirit." Then he shook the branch above our heads and began to chant: "Peace. Pax. Pace. Shalom."

I waited for Ange to come up with the appropriately evolved reply, but she just grinned uncomfortably as the holly leaves drifted down around her head, so I tried to recall my own countercultural days back in the 1960s, when alternative-style introspective catchphrases effortlessly rolled off our tongues. But the best I could come up with was, "How's it hangin'?"

That's when Gina spotted us and waved us over.

"Love your store," I told her as she gave Angie a hug.

"Really?" she skeptically replied. "I didn't think this was your cup of tea."

"I'm a man of many interests," I countered.

"You're also the man who microwaved the alternative holiday CD I brought to Uncle Mario's party last December."

"You can't prove that was me," I said, though of course it was. I cooked it good, and I gotta tell you, I savor the moment still—watching through the little microwave window as *A Very Druid Christmas* rotated slowly, curling at the edges and steaming like a potato chip just out of the fryer.

"Sixteen bucks that CD cost me," carped Gina. "I'd just bought it that day."

"Oh, sorry," I commiserated, "and you only got to play it, what, twenty-seven times in a row?"

Gina scowled, then lifted a tiny bottle from the Aromatherapy rack and handed it to Angie.

"It's petunia oil," she said. "A natural tension reliever. Say there's a constant, grating, unavoidable irritation in your immediate environment. This stuff numbs the nerve ends and soothes away stress. I can get it to you in fifty-five-gallon drums."

Then Gina led Angie off to have her aura photographed, and I was left to browse. I listened to tapes of whales singing. I looked at books about angelic intercessions and ancient Navajo rites. There was a discussion on herbal remedies, some Reiki massage, some regression therapy, and a big silver plate of plump miniature weenies.

My first stop was at the Books of Wisdom table, where I saw featured works by Carl Jung, Lao-Tzu, Saint

Teresa of Avila, and Black Elk, the famous medicine man of the Oglala Sioux.

"Can I help you?" asked a nice young neo-hippie, type clerk named Monica. I wasn't really looking to buy, but I figured, what the heck, a good book is always worth the money. "What have you got by the Amazing Kreskin?" I inquired.

Monica smiled and said she'd go check, but twenty minutes later she had not returned, so I decided to mingle. The place was packed with all sorts of interesting-looking people, and being a congenitally gregarious type, I tried to strike up relevant conversations with random passers-by.

"Hey," I'd offer, "how about that Shroud of Turin? Like to have some bath towels hold up that well, know what I'm saying?"

But that got me nowhere, so I walked over to the folks at the Miracle of Hemp booth and tried to break the ice with a joke.

"Hey," I cried, "have any of you guys heard about this new, simplified Eastern religion for people who can't handle the transcendent subtleties of Buddhism? It's called, 'Gee, I Can't Believe It's Not Buddha'!"

Ba-Da-Bing! Nothing.

Then a shapely priestess of the Wicca religion draped in sheer, gauzy robes happened by, and in what I thought was an inspired "Wayne's World" takeoff, I thrust my hips comically in her direction while shouting, "Feng-shui! Feng-shui!"

That's when the security guy started eyeballing me, so I decided to move along to the Near Death Experience exhibit, but as I walked toward the lecture hall I spotted a stairway leading down to what was clearly a small basement workshop.

I had a decision to make: To my left was documented evidence of spiritual immortality; to my right, a chance to fool with somebody else's tools.

Well, I figured, heaven can wait.

As it turned out, Gina's tool kit was skimpy, but she had a nice big worktable and plenty of storage space. What caught my eye, though, was the network of hairline cracks riddling the masonry foundation walls. Tiny cracks like these pose no structural danger, of course, but left unattended, they can give moisture and insects easy access to your home. So I decided, what with the new millennium and all, that I'd bury the hatchet with Gina and magnanimously fix all the cracks.

It's a simple job. First, you widen the crack with an old chisel or flat-bladed screwdriver, then you give the crack a stiff wire-brushing to chase out all the debris. When the prep work's done, you mix up a batch of patching mortar (ask at the hardware store for the right stuff for the job), moisten the crack with a little water, press some mortar into the crack, then smooth it over with a trowel.

Problem was, I was far from my trusty tools, and I had to make do with what Gina had on hand. I couldn't find a chisel, but I did dig up what looked like a petrified walrus tusk (probably an Inuit good-luck trinket), which performed quite nicely as a scraper, and an Iroquois headdress made from a porcupine pelt, with which I scrubbed the little crevasses clean. In minutes, all the cracks were gouged out and ready for mortar.

But a vigorous search of the storage area turned up no mortar whatsoever, and I was about to make a quick hardware store run, when I spotted, on the worktable, an ornate metal box filled with a gray, cementatious powder. I sifted the powder through my fingertips. It felt right. I mixed in a little water. The consistency looked good. I pulled a credit card from my wallet and used it as a putty knife to slather some of the paste into one of the cracks on the wall. It went on like a dream: good adhesion, excellent finish qualities.

So I set to work in earnest, and in less than half an hour, I had patched over most of the cracks. That's when the two monks in saffron robes came down the stairs. They walked to the worktable. They furiously glanced around.

"Wherever is the Baba?" asked the short one.

"On this I cannot say," replied the taller guy. "Here is the very spot exactly upon which I placed him."

I cleared my throat to let them know I was there. "I've been down here half an hour," I said. "Haven't seen your friend Bubba."

The monks turned to face me. They gasped when they saw the metal box in my hand. The short monk fainted. The tall one pointed at the box and began to shriek. "Stop immediately without delay! Whatever are you thinking in your mind to be doing such a thing!?"

"I'm sorry," I said. "Is this your mortar?"

"You are a blundering idiot without question!" cried the tall monk. "That is not mortar of any sort, certainly. It is the ashes of the Great Baba with which you are horribly plastering the wall!"

"Come again?"

"The Baba! Our spiritual leader whose ashes were to be enshrined today in this place of enlightenment where the faithful could revere him always. Now it is not possible to revere him at all, as you have reduced him to a very sad glob of pasty mud and pressed him so tightly into these tiny cracking places!!!"

I set down the mortar, shook the goo from my fingers, and gave the monk an apologetic shrug. "You wouldn't have a Kleenex?" I inquired.

The monk gasped in horror, then ran upstairs. Working frantically, I scooped as much of the Baba as I could out of the wall cracks and pressed him back into the pretty little box. Then I went upstairs, where I found the angry monk whispering to a glaring crowd of surly true believers, and tried to calm things down.

"Okay," I said, holding up the box, "the Baba is back in his final resting place. Most of him, anyway."

An ugly murmuring spread through the crowd, and someone pointed at my lapel, where a small gray dollop of Baba resided. I scooped up the blob with a fingertip and scraped it into the box, wiped my finger on my pants, then gently placed the little casket on a nearby table, beside the Pyramid Power display. I'm sure everyone noticed, as I did, that the box was slowly leaking.

"Okay," I advised, "he's going to be a little soupy for a while, so I'd give him a good twenty-four hours to cure. But once he sets up," I said, "he's good for eternity."

The crowd began inching forward. The incensed monk was leading the way. "You have desecrated the memory of the Baba," he said.

"Hey, whoa, hold on there, folks," I pleaded. "Let's not forget, we are all one. We're all seekers of wisdom and peace. I mean, what would the Baba do if he was in your shoes?"

"What did he say?" asked someone in the crowd.

"He says he has Baba on his shoes!!" someone answered.

"Defiler!" someone shouted. "Ghoul!" cried someone else.

They were backing me into a corner now, cutting off all routes of escape, and I realized, as I hastily scanned the crowd, that they were arming themselves as they advanced. Some snatched heavy crystal balls from display racks. Others picked up ceremonial Apache tomahawks, or the long wooden-headed drumsticks Chinese sorcerers use to smack their big brass gongs. I retreated slowly, groping behind me as they backed me into a corner and up against the Aromatherapy rack.

Then an idea struck me. I whirled around and frantically searched the display case until I found an economy-size bottle of just what I needed. I screwed off the lid and doused the crowd with the fragrant liquid inside.

"Ewwwwww," someone complained, "what was that stuff?"

"That's petunia oil," I replied. "It soothes the spirit. So breathe deep. In no time, you people will all be your old, mellow, placid selves again, and we'll be able to talk this over sensibly."

There was silence, then a chorus of guffaws.

"Right," shouted someone in the back of the mob, "like we buy that aromatherapy bull for like a minute."

They laughed hilariously for a moment, then they continued their slow advance. I had to think clearly. Whatever was about to converge, would converge on me, and it would not be harmonic. My only chance was the time-tested tactic of diversion.

"Look!" I said, pointing to the rear of the room. "It's Yanni!"

The crowd gasped and turned as one, and in that split second I dashed past them like a church mouse scurrying along the baseboard; then I darted through a set of double doors and hauled ashes toward daylight.

The mob recovered quickly and gave chase, but thanks largely to the prominent gluteus maximus muscles that are the hereditary hallmark of the Agita clan, they were no match for me in the open field. I pulled away easily as I vaulted the serene Japanese sand garden and splashed through the miniature Zen reflection pool. Then I hotfooted it through the fire walkers' workshop, bolted out the back door, and sprinted straight home.

It was already dark when Angela walked in an hour later.

"What do you have to say for yourself?" she said. "Gina almost had a riot on her hands."

"I was just trying to help," I answered. "How was I supposed to know that was a holy man's cremated remains? I mean, they basically had him in an ashtray."

"You were trespassing in Gina's workshop," said Ange.

"I was doing her a favor."

"You were meddling where you didn't belong."

"Like I begged you to take me there."

"I should be able to take you places," she said. "And I shouldn't have to worry that you'll sneak off and start getting handy. This is just another case of these crazy handy impulses causing problems."

"That's an exaggeration."

"How about the Buttermans' party last month?" Angie said. "You got bored and disappeared for an hour?"

"They had paint crumbling from the old wainscoting in the bathroom," I said. "It could have been lead based, they have small kids . . . I saw a handy need."

"So you sanded it all down to bare wood and slapped on a fresh coat of primer. . . ."

"Took me forty-five minutes, tops."

"But the paint wasn't old and it wasn't lead based, was it? It wasn't even flaking. It was *crackled*. An antiquing technique. The Buttermans paid a lot of money to have a decorative artist create that effect by hand."

"And you approve of that?" I asked.

"The Buttermans have excellent taste," said Angie.

"It's a perversion of handy values," I said, "this alarming trend toward intentionally making things look distressed and decrepit—faux crackled paint, faux crumbling plaster, faux dingy woodwork. I mean, what's next, faux termite infestations? Faux leaky toilets?"

Ange crossed her arms and silently drummed her fingers on her forearms.

"I want you to call Gina and apologize," she said.

"Apologize?" I complained. "I was almost lynched."

"Are you going to call her?"

"Absolutely not," I said.

Angie's glare was withering.

"Well, let me sleep on it, okay?"

"Fine," said Ange, storming up the staircase, "but you aren't sleeping anywhere near me." Moments later, pillows, sheets, and blankets came tumbling down the steps.

"Sweet dreams!" she shouted as she slammed the bedroom door.

Wearily, I gathered up the bedclothes and trudged off to the den, but there I found Alphonse, my beloved cat, stretched out blissfully on the sofa in deep feline slumber. I poked his pudgy stomach, but he didn't rouse. I tapped him on the head. He only rolled to his side, stretched luxuriously, and began to softly snore.

I couldn't bear to disturb him, so I dragged myself off to the basement and bedded down on the lumpy old sofa over by the Maytag. But I knew I wouldn't sleep. I never sleep well when Ange isn't near me. I miss her soft heft on the mattress beside me; I miss the gentle heave of her sleeping body as she rolls lightly from side to side; I miss the cute little nasal clicks she emits, like the call of a baby dolphin, when the room air gets too dry. . . .

Plus, I had to share the basement with that horrific throng of damaged gnomes, which were scattered across the floor like a battalion of diminutive war wounded, waiting for triage. I know they're just made of plaster, but seriously, some of those severed heads looked like they were really holding a grudge.

7 Banished

ow is the winter of my discontent, made even more wintry because I'm sleeping in the basement surrounded by a plug-ugly army of gnomes.

Two weeks now, I've spent my nights in this dark and drafty basement, with only my cheery lava lamp collection and my Spike Jones albums to leaven the gloom. It's the handyman thing, of course, which has once again punched Angie's hot button and led her to banish me to this desolate basement exile. Happens every time one of my ambitious handy projects goes awry. I don't know how things look to others, but from my point of view, I think she's a little quick to pull the trigger. So many things set her off. Say, for example, I slip and tumble while shingling the porch roof and crumple the canvas rag top of her cousin's teensy red Miata; or my new pneumatic nail gun twitches off a clip or two and pulverizes a certain neighbor's gaggle of pet plaster gnomes.

Yes, to be sure, there have been low points, but hey, I'm a trailblazer over here. I'm pushing the handy envelope to see how far it'll stretch. Sure I could follow the standard procedures, color inside the lines, act like one of those butt-smooching handy-gurus proliferating all over PBS and cable. But those guys are selling you a lie. In their sugar-coated handy world, nails never bend, boards never split, you never staple your sleeve to a stud, you never wall up Mrs. Plumpton's wandering geriatric schnauzer and have to tear down a weekend's worth of Sheetrocking to set him free.

I can't be like those TV guys; I gotta be me. But society doesn't like it when you follow your own way. Controversy rises. Ask Gandhi. Ask Elvis. It's not easy when you're trying just to be you.

Ange has heard this rant before, but she remains steadfastly unmoved by the demands of my offbeat handy calling. She refuses to embrace the vision.

Instead, she is compelled, by the fierce, ancient instincts of her proud Sicilian forebears, to take out her frustrations on my hide. Hence, these many midnights dark and dreary spent all by my lonesome in this drafty, gnome-infested cellar.

But I don't want you to think I'm feeling sorry for myself. In fact, I'm trying to make productive use of my time down here. I'm passing the lonely hours with pen in hand, capturing my deepest thoughts on paper.

Another whiny jailhouse memoir? Have no fear, that's not the Agita way. Instead, I've decided to do something for the children, so I'm creating a new line of reality-based kids' books, which will cut through the condescendingly cloying crap that has always flooded the juvenile bookshelves. These books will not jerk kids around with some sanitized, fuzzy-bunny version of life. They'll be tougher, edgier, and uncompromisingly honest. And they'll wise kids up quickly as to what really makes this cold, cruel world go 'round. Here are some selected titles:

1. *The Little Engine That Could Give a Rat's Ass*
2. *Breaking Wind in the Willows*
3. *Winnie-the-Prick*
4. *Where's That Lardbutt Waldo?*

In the meanwhile, I am working hard to smooth things out with Angie. For instance, I've given up those late-night Tang and Cheetos binges, since Ange says nutrition might be affecting my moods. I threw out all my glossy tool catalogs (I buy them for the articles, but Ange calls it handy porn). And I tried that trick where you slip a rubber band over your wrist and snap it hard each time you have an unwanted impulse. (Actually, that kept the handy urges at bay rather effectively, but Ange made me take it off when she realized I was starting to crave the luscious little sting.)

Through it all, I struggled mightily to be good. Ange realized this, I think, and it softened her feelings toward me. For example, one morning, when she came down to the basement to wake me, she found me sitting up on the sofa, still fast asleep, sawing at thin air with an invisible saw. I was making rhythmic zee-zah-zee-zah noises, she says, and my face was a picture of innocent bliss.

"I know things are hard for you right now," she said when she woke me from the dream. "Just remind yourself that you're learning to trade immediate gratification for a more meaningful, long-term kind of happiness."

Seeing that her words confused me, Ange smiled and mentally reconnoitered. "We'll work on that long-term concept later," she said. "The important thing now is that you need to learn restraint, so you can resist that crazy little handyman inside. He's not your friend, Vinnie. He only wants to lead you astray."

"The little handyman is persuasive," I whispered. "The little handyman is fun."

Ange sat on the sofa and took my hands in hers.

"You have to make a choice," she said. "It's the little handyman, or it's me. . . ."

My face crumpled involuntarily, and for a second I thought I was going to cry. For some reason, I pictured Angie in the clingy black mesh body stocking I bought for her last Christmas. Then, in a twisted trick of the mind, I saw the same outfit being modeled on a runway by the little inner handyman. The little handyman, it turns out, looks a lot like Gene Shalit. And oh, what an image I now shall carry to the grave.

"It's so hard, Ange," I whimpered. "The little handy bastard won't stop pushing."

"You need to quiet him down," said Angie. "Here's a trick that might help. When my mind is agitated and confused, I sit quietly for a few moments and visualize a peaceful scene. Maybe a crystal blue mountain lake with snow-capped peaks in the distance, or a graceful waterfall tumbling into a tropical lagoon. It calms the spirit and settles the mind. Go ahead, try it."

I closed me eyes. "I see sailboats on a pond," I said.

"Good," she said. "Anything else?"

"I smell fragrant fields of wildflowers."

"That sounds perfect. What do you hear?"

"I hear that heavenly music at the beginning of *The Simpsons.*"

"Well, whatever," said Ange. "How does it all make you feel?"

"Calm. Very calm," I answered, lying through my teeth. In fact, all I'd seen was what I always see when I close my eyes—thousands of handy challenges going unanswered. I saw hairline cracks in the bedroom walls, I heard the maddening drip of the powder-room faucet, I felt the floorboards in the den sag and squeal beneath my feet, and worst of all, I saw my backyard project languishing in limbo and the whole damn house falling into chaos and decay as I sat helplessly on the sidelines, forbidden to respond. The frustration was crushing. The boredom was driving me insane. What I needed, more than anything, was to feel productive, even if in a nonhandy capacity. I needed a harmless pastime to fill my empty hours with activity and drive the handy urges from my mind—a kind of methadone therapy for my handy jones.

So I waited until later that afternoon, and sounded out Angie on the topic.

"Maybe I'll set up a small kiln out in the yard and fire up some homemade Hummelware," I told her. "That's not technically handy."

Ange looked up glumly from her *Cosmo*. "No, Vinnie," she muttered, "no kilns."

I spun on my heels slowly, and thoughtfully stroked my chin. "Can I have a chemistry set?" I asked.

"Forget it," she said.

"Just a thought," I said, chuckling. "Hey, Ange . . . how about a perm?"

Angie tossed her magazine on the coffee table and rose from the couch with a scowl. "I'm going for a walk," she said. "If you need to feel productive, why don't you fix the gnomes?"

"I'm out of weatherproof epoxy," I fibbed. "It's special stuff. I order it over the Internet, from this Garden Gnome Web site I found—www.gnomedepot.com."

"Then, I don't know," grumbled Angie as she stepped out the door. "Clean the closets, bake some cookies."

I nodded happily and raced to the stove. I made

2,397 nut rolls, after which I mixed some batter in a washtub and made a single lemon bar that weighed 387 pounds. That got my juices going, and soon I was struck by a blinding inspiration for a monumental piece of confectionery installation art—I would bake an army of life-size gingerbread men and stack them in military ranks in the basement, like those terra-cotta soldiers they found in that ancient Chinese tomb. It wasn't handiness per se, but it would create a sensation, and I'd be a cinch for the cover of the *Smithsonian*. Then, maybe, Ange would see me in a different light.

Unfortunately, just as the guys from the baker's supply had erected the conveyor belt and were starting to unload the semi, Ange came home and made me go lie down.

But it was too late. I had tasted the old thrill of creation, of getting something done, and now I felt the handy beast inside me growing stronger. I was having chills and sudden hot flashes. I needed to get handy. I needed to get well.

Ange told me there'd be times like this, so I wrapped myself in blankets and sweated it out. All night I slipped in and out of nightmares, I yammered deliriously, I clawed in agony at the Herculon nubble of the basement couch.

And by morning, I felt stronger, more stable. I felt the monkey slipping from my back. I even got a couple of the gnomes glued back together. Then Ange came home with that damn little table, and everything slid straight to hell.

8
The Shaky Table

I t happened on a Saturday morning. I was doing my best to gulp down a big steaming breakfast mug of a grain-based coffee alternative called Postum—part of Angie's nutritional stress-reduction plan—when Ange herself burst in, brandishing her latest flea market find.

"Look at this!" she shouted, holding up a rickety long-legged lamp table that looked like a refugee from the local dump. "A genuine shaky table!" she cried. "And I got it for a song!"

When she set it down in the corner, I walked over and gave the little table a gentle shove. It wobbled and staggered on its spindly legs like a two-day old giraffe.

"It's shaky, all right," I allowed her.

It was homely too. The chipped red paint was dull and grimy. The wood was riddled with wormholes and dents. A wide, ugly crack ran across the badly warped top, and the legs were all uneven. But my sweet funny Ange had fallen in love with this little ugly duckling, so I kept my opinions to myself.

"I can't believe I found this at a neighborhood flea market," cried Angie, her smile lighting up the room. "I've always wanted a table just like this. But shaky stuff is so hard to find."

I felt a little sorry for her right then, but it made me love her even more.

"Get your own lunch, Vincent," she said, racing back out the door. "I'm going to buy some fresh flowers for the table. And I need the perfect vase. And maybe a nice lace doily. Oh, wait till I tell my sister. She loves shaky furniture too."

Then she dashed out the door, and frankly, not a moment too soon, because all this shaky talk was starting to annoy me.

So I turned to have another chuckle over the sorry little bundle of sticks in the corner, but when I laid eyes on the table again, chills ran down my spine. Suddenly, I saw what I'd been left alone with—pure lurid temptation: a searing siren call of yearning handy need. Oh, the nearness of it, the enticing opportunities it called to mind. Leering at the little table, with desire and self-loathing slugging it out in my soul, I felt exuberant and despicable all at once, the way that moral cretin

Humbert Humbert must have felt the first time he laid eyes on the scandalously provocative nymphet Lolita.

"Resist," I said out loud, but the lure of the table was strong, and my thoughts soon grew jumbled and jittery. Perversely, I began to convince myself that in her heart of hearts, Ange really wanted me to fix the little table. Obviously, she loved the sad little thing, so why else would she leave me alone with it? Who knows my compulsions better than she? Why, it was practically an invitation.

Oh, the torment in my soul. I knew it was the handy madness talking. I knew I had to clear my mind. So I closed my eyes and tried to soothe my surging urges with the visualization techniques Ange had taught me. I made myself breathe deep and even while I pictured a charming Alpine village on a placid mountain lake, and a serene, snow-capped mountain peak rising in the distance.

And what do you know, it was working! My heartbeat slowed. My eye stopped twitching. It was all very pleasant, really: I could smell the scent of the pine forest, and taste crisp bright snowflakes melting on my tongue.

But then the earth trembled, the pine trees began to thrash, and with a deafening roar, the top of the mountain exploded. I watched in horror as volcanic ash spewed from the gaping crater, and rivers of molten lava began to stream down the slopes. All the little chalets were bursting into flame. The lake was starting to boil. Chubby little guys in lederhosen were screaming, and scrambling for their lives.

"Who am I kidding?" I shouted as I drove the image from my mind. "I need to fix something, now!" In a dark fury, I grabbed the table, whisked it off to my workshop, and vigorously set to work.

Oh, what a handy rush as I revved up my belt sander and scoured the table's finish down to bare, virginal wood. I wish you could have been there, because everything was clicking. I was at the very top of my game. It helped, of course, that furniture fix-ups are among the most satisfying tasks a do-it-yourselfer can tackle. The results are so clear and immediate. And the techniques aren't difficult at all.

For example, say you have some ugly dents in a wooden tabletop. Those dents happened because something heavy struck the table and forced the wood fibers to compress. All you need to do is to plump up those pinched fibers and the dent will disappear as if by legerdemain.

Here's the drill: Place a damp cloth over the dent, then press the cloth lightly with an ordinary steam iron set on high. The dented wood fibers will absorb the moisture from the cloth and swell back to their normal configuration. Presto! What dent? You see a dent?

And here's a cheap, easy fix for small cracks in wood furniture: First, swipe some wood-toned crayons from your kids and melt them down in an old saucepan, mixing different colors until you get a shade that matches your wood. When the liquid has cooled into a soft paste, press it firmly into the crack. Wait for the patch to harden, then shave it flush with a sharp chisel, and buff the surface briskly with a soft cloth until the patch blends with the surrounding finish. (You can also use tiny balls of softened crayon to plug small pit marks and nail holes in the wood.)

What about veneered furniture? Veneering is a time-honored practice in which thin sheets of a fine hardwood are glued over a stable base of a cheaper, humbler wood. Nothing wrong with that; even very valuable antiques sport veneered surfaces. But because veneers are so thin, they require special handling when problems arise.

Say, for example, there's a bulging blister the size of a quarter on the top of a veneered dresser. Blisters happen when the glue fails, and the veneer loosens from its base. The goal is to glue it back down again, as uninvasively as possible.

For starters, try the steam iron trick again. Lay a damp cloth across the blister, and press lightly with the iron. The hope here is that the heat of the iron will turn the dried-up glue all gooey once again while the steam softens the warped veneer and allows you to press it down into the newly rejuvenated glue. Just be sure to work gently, and be patient. Warped veneer can turn brittle, so wait until the steam softens up the veneer before applying any pressure.

With any luck, you can literally iron away that blister. But sometimes the old glue is just too far gone. In that case, fill a small hypodermic needle with wood glue (you can buy the needles at craft stores) and inject the glue under the skin of the blister. Use the iron to soften the veneer and press it down into the fresh glue, then cover the repair with a wood block and weight it down with bricks and let the new glue dry overnight.

Very simple, really. But some blisters in veneer are too large for such simple remedies. These stubborn blisters have to go under the knife, a challenging repair that I find quite fulfilling.

The first step is to slit the blister lengthwise with a very sharp razor knife. Next use the steam iron trick to soften the blistered veneer, and when it's pliable, work a little wood glue all under the blister with the blade of the razor knife. Now, press down the repair with a wallpaper seam roller, then slap a strip of adhesive tape over the incision to keep it from opening as it dries. (Don't forget to weight it all down with the wood-block-and-brick procedure.)

See what I mean? You don't have to live with dinged and dented furniture. All it takes is a little patience, a few tools, and a soul full of handy love.

Speaking of which, it took all the handy love I could muster to rescue Angie's table. After I'd sanded it smooth, I patched all the cracks and gouges, sawed the legs even, and glued up the wobbly joints. A few coats of quick-dry polyurethane and a high-speed power buffing gave the sweet little table a dazzling, bowling alley sheen. It took all day to finish, and I had just set it back in place when Angie came home, with a bundle of packages in her arms.

"Vincent," she said, in an oddly quiet voice. "What the hell is that?"

"It's the shaky table," I told her, "except it's not shaky anymore. It's rock solid." To prove the point, I hopped over to it and beat out a drum roll on the top.

Ange crossed her arms and stared at me. "It's not a *shaky* table," she muttered, "it's a *Shaker* table. It's a hundred and fifty years old! It's never been repaired or tampered with—it still had its original coat of paint!"

"It needed some freshening up, all righty," I said, chuckling. "But, heck, look at it now. You couldn't tell this baby from a brand-spanking-new one down at Ethan Allen."

Angie dropped her packages. She lurched forward and grabbed me by the lapel. Then she let me go and stormed toward the door. Then she spun around and made another aggressive advance, but she broke it off at the last moment and, with an anguished groan, raised her hands to the heavens then stomped up the stairs.

She didn't come down until way after dark. When she did, she didn't look happy.

"Sit!" she barked, pointing at the couch. I promptly obeyed. She slapped a business card on the coffee table. It read:

NICHOLAS J. RUFFALFALO, Ph.D.
INDIVIDUAL AND FAMILY COUNSELING
2020 Redwood Lane

Ange crossed her arms and waited for my reaction. I had to think fast. So I nodded reflectively as I examined the business card, then, with a startled look on my face, I dropped the card and leapt to my feet.

"Holy cow," I shouted, pointing out the window, "is that a full moon? That means the car is way overdue for an oil change! Thank God there's an all-night Jiffy Lube at the other end of the county—"

"Freeze!" said Angie as I made for the door. "We're going to have this conversation."

"But, geeze, Ange," I said, "we've been through all this before. You know I don't believe in shrinks. All that opening up and being vulnerable and messing around down in the dark places. Yuck. I mean, who cares how long a guy was breast-fed, or how many times he dreams about the train and the tunnel, or why he used to feel so giddy when he'd parade around in his Aunt Rita's red satin pumps—"

"Vincent?"

"I'm talking theoretically," I pointed out. "Anyway, there's nothing here for a shrink to sink his teeth into. I'm just not that complicated. What you see is what you get."

I spread my arms wide and smiled innocently to drive home my point. Ange didn't seem to be buying.

"Not complicated?" said Angie. "The guy with the gnome phobia? The guy who thinks my sweet old aunt is a witch?"

"That doesn't make me a nutcake," I said. "It just means I'm vigilant."

"You have to call Dr. Ruffalfalo," said Ange.

"Let me mull it over," I said.

"There's nothing to mull," she answered. "This is crisis intervention; you no longer have a vote."

"At least give me some time to get used to the idea," I implored.

"You have all night," she said. "But if you don't call him in the morning, I will."

Then she went to bed, and I made my way down to the sad little basement sofa. I slipped on my pj's, threw a tarp over that ghastly gaggle of gnomes, and crawled under the covers. I felt Ange was being unfair. How about seeing things from my position for once? After all, there I was, with my marriage full of conflict and tension, my deepest handy urges stifled, my future uncertain, and my basic sense of purpose and identity hopelessly muddled.

See what I'm saying? At times like this, who can concentrate on therapy?

9
Breaking and Entering

Greetings from the big house. The calaboose. The slammer. The can. That's right. I, Vinnie Agita, am "in the system" doing time for the crime of being handy. But I should be out of here in a few hours, as soon as Mrs. Agita has had her little laugh.

Actually, I'm in a holding cell at the local precinct house, waiting to be bailed. The deputy here, Burt, is a burly guy with a whopping paunch hanging over his gun belt, and for a joke I've been calling him Barney. "Hey, Barney, how's Floyd the Barber?" "Hey, Barney, getting anywhere with that waitress babe Thelma Lou?" That sort of thing.

At first he just glared at me, and I feared my well-intentioned irony might have offended him. But then he came over and leaned his beefy forearms on the bars of my cell. "Wanna know the difference between me and Barney Fife?" he said. "Well, see, Barney had a little .22 pistol and one little bullet. Whereas I have this 9mm automatic here on my hip that can fire 3.5 hollow-point rounds per second, each one of which can make a hole in a man the size of a baseball." And then he chuckled and walked away, so I knew he was enjoying the banter.

By the way, I'm innocent, of course; the hapless victim of a bizarre and tragic series of events. It started early this morning, which dawned all drizzly and sullen. My mind, which usually requires no more than six or seven mugs of java to buzz like a beehive full of handy inspiration, felt bruised and sullen and mushy, like an overripe melon. I needed a jump start; I needed a chore; I needed something to give meaning to the end-lessly sprawling day that lay ahead. So I decided to, you know, burglarize my own house.

Brilliant concept, no? I mean, what better way to flush out weaknesses in your home's security than to subject your defenses to the canny wiles of a master thief, such as *moi?*

So I went into seclusion with a stack of home secu-rity books to bone up on the fine art of breaking and entering. I studied tools, techniques, and defenses. I pored over police reports and case histories, and as the hours passed, I felt myself evolving into a cool, cunning master of B&E, a light-fingered shadow of the night, with larceny in my heart and a pry bar down my Dockers.

It scared me, to tell the truth, how easily I slipped into this felonious persona. It was as if a door had opened to some dark, dishonest corner of my mind and I found my thoughts melded to a million thieving minds. In that instant, I knew their secrets, their fears, their tactics; I walked their walk, I talked their talk. In my mind, see, I became a larcenous land-pirate for an evening. Then I waited for nightfall and a-pilfering I did go.

Now, of course, you're wondering how you can keep creeps like me from dropping by. Well, my colleagues and I tend to look for the easiest mark, so we love dark yards and thick bushes, which give us cover as we work. We appreciate it when you leave your doors and windows unlocked, let mail and newspapers pile up, and burn your porch lights 'round the clock while you're on vacation.

But you've heard all that before, so now I want to focus on one crucial aspect of home security—something you depend upon as a primary barrier between you and me: your home's exterior doors.

That stout front door, for example, may look like a bulwark to you, but really, even when it's locked, all that stands between you and plunder are a few square inches of wood and steel. Think about it: A door is made to swing open, and with a little encouragement from me, that's exactly what it will do. It's no surprise, really, that eighty percent of all break-ins involve a door.

While we're talking doors, let's take a moment to discuss your locks. First off, if your doors are guarded only by the flimsy locks in the doorknobs, or those surface-mounted locks that have spring-action latches, you can instantly improve your home's security right now by simply stacking all your valuables in the front yard.

Believe me, anything less than a sturdy dead-bolt lock is no lock at all. A dead-bolt lock has a sturdy "cylinder" set into the door, which contains the keyhole and the mechanism that pushes the thick steel "bolt" in and out of the door when you turn the key. When you lock the door, the bolt slides into a hole in the door frame surrounded by a metal "strike plate." When the bolt's in the strike plate, the door is secure and everything's ducky, and ducky it shall remain until I get that irresistible hankerin' for all your portable electronics, because even the hardiest dead bolt can be defeated.

Here's what I do: When I find a likely target—a house with an older wooden door that's shielded from view—I case the joint for a while, then, when the coast seems clear, I run up and deliver a good swift kick. This usually splinters the wood around the cylinder, or tears the dead bolt and strike plate out of the door frame, so that the door swings open, and I step inside.

Kick-ins are a favorite method of forced entry, but they can be noisy, so sometimes I'll slip my thin-bladed pry bar between the edge of the door and the door frame and "jimmy" it sharply sideways, which bends the door frame just enough so that the dead bolt pops out of the strike.

Sounds easy, huh? In most cases it is. In fact, there's probably no way to keep a determined burglar from breaking through your door. But fortunately for you, we light-fingered types aren't motivated by a deep work ethic, so all you need to do, really, is make our jobs a little harder and in most cases we'll lose interest and go away.

One way to make our jobs very hard is to install steel doors. They don't splinter, and if you fit the door frame with reinforced strike plates (something every door should have), they're very resistant to kick-ins.

If you don't like the look of steel doors, you can beef up your wooden door with a variety of metal reinforcers. These are usually thin brass sleeves that wrap around the door edge and the lock cylinder, helping that crucial part of the door withstand a kick-in attack.

To guard against jimmying, make sure your doors fit snugly in their frames, and think about installing a "jimmy plate." This is a metal strip that, when bolted to the door, prevents me from wedging my pry bar into position. Also, make sure your dead bolt has at least a one-inch "throw"—the depth to which it penetrates the frame—so it can't be so easily popped out of the strike. Dead-bolt "rim locks" are another good option: In these burly locks, the dead bolt slides vertically between two sets of overlapping steel knuckles, which makes them very hard to jimmy.

There are other ways a savvy brigand like myself can slip through your doorway, and corresponding ways you can slow me down. Sometimes I'll pry back the door frame just enough to slip a saw blade through and simply hack through the dead bolt. But that won't work if your dead bolt has little steel rollers inside. (The rollers spin, preventing the saw teeth from biting.) If your lock cylinder protrudes from the door, I can grasp it with big locking pliers and simply twist it out of the hole. (You can thwart that move by installing a lock encased in a loose metal sheath that turns harmlessly when I twist.) Some of my more accomplished colleagues can deftly pick your locks, but there are high-security locks on the market whose tricky guts are virtually pick-proof. And finally, if I feel like it, I'll just drill out the lock cylinder, or beat it to submission with a hammer. Your best defense here is to make sure your lock is crafted of "case-hardened steel," and that it bears the "UL" seal of approval. That means that in independent tests by Underwriters Laboratories, the lock has withstood at least five to ten minutes of burglar-type abuse, and believe me, I don't want to be drilling or pounding on your door for any longer than that.

So it's pretty simple: The tougher your door, the more likely I am to select another victim. My nightmare scenario: a steel door in a tight steel frame with a state-of-the-art dead bolt attached. Provide yourself such a portal and you could leave the Hope diamond out on the coffee table and still sleep soundly at night. Except, of course, for all those nice, inviting windows.

It's true. We burglars like nothing better than a flimsy door, but we'll settle for a vulnerable window anytime. Doesn't take a Braniac to understand why: Anything made out of glass that's designed to slide or lift or crank open is not exactly a bank vault door.

Take your common double-hungs, for example. Many have only old-fashioned butterfly locks securing the sashes. I can open those babies with a butter knife and a flick of the wrist. Newer, stronger sash locks may thwart the butter knife trick, but a pry bar slipped under the lower sash and jimmied hard will force the sash upward, popping those locks like bottle caps. Wouldn't even wake you up. You'll still be in your REM phase, and I'll be pulling the family jewels from that hollow ceramic cantaloupe in the fridge. (Nice try, but we know all the hiding places.)

There are all sorts of sturdy window locks on the market that can make double-hung windows highly resistant to jimmying, and most employ the basic principle of blocking the window's natural tendency to slide open.

Here's a simple, cheap, and effective version. First, close the window. Then, using a $5/16$-inch bit, drill holes in the upper corners of the lower sash, where the two sashes overlap. Drill all the way through the lower sash and partway through the upper. Now you can slip a $1/4$-inch steel bolt into the hole and the two sashes just can't be pried open.

You can elaborate on this concept. Some folks cut

off the bolt head flush with the sash so that even if the window glass is broken the would-be intruder can't simply reach in and pull out the bolt. (The bolts can be drawn out with strong bar magnets, which you should keep near each bolted window.) And if you drill more holes in the lower sash, you can even bolt the window in a slightly open position.

By the way, DO NOT try this technique on windows with vinyl or metal sashes. Instead, buy a keyed window lock, which clamps onto the side channels of the window to prevent the sashes from sliding.

What about casement windows? These are generally a little tougher than double-hungs, because their metal cranking mechanisms make them difficult to wrench open. But if a thief breaks the glass, all he need do is reach in and crank himself a welcome. So it makes sense to remove those crank handles and store them safely out of reach. If you have casements in an especially vulnerable location—or any windows you'd really like to harden up—think about replacing the window glass with a tough synthetic glazing, like Lexan, which is virtually unbreakable.

While you're at it, give some thought to protecting your basement windows. Bars are effective. They're also ugly and depressing. Glass blocks are a good option. They're tough, they let in lots of light, and in the right places, they really don't look half bad.

Keep in mind, though, that you'll never make your windows invulnerable. You're goal, instead, is to make the bad guy's job tough enough that he'll just move on to easier pickins. . . .

That was my frame of mind exactly when I first laid eyes on the Agita homestead and slyly cased the joint from across the street. I didn't like the looks of things at first: two bright porch lights were burning and the door was in plain view of passersby. Then I slipped down the driveway and into the backyard, which was dark and cozy and private. "Well, all right," I whispered in satisfaction. "I smell VCR."

When my eyes had adjusted to the darkness I took a look around. On my left was a tall basement window of impregnable glass block, but in the shadows to my right the basement door—old, wooden, shielded from view—looked downright tasty. I stepped forward, quietly grasped the knob, and gave the door a quick butt with my shoulder. It felt surprisingly beefy and resolute. Must be a thick one. Definitely not kick-in material. So I pulled out my pry bar and tried to slip it between the door and the frame, hoping to pry back the frame just enough to pop the lock's dead bolt free from the strike. Alas, a metal guard, firmly screwed to the door edge, denied the pry bar's entry.

Stymied, I stepped back to consider my options. The only other reasonable point of entry—a pair of double-hung windows in the den—was a hopeless fifteen feet above the ground. I had to face it, this caper was a bust. But as I turned to leave, I spotted an extension ladder lying beside the garage. This was a bit of serendipity too sweet to refuse, and moments later the ladder was in place and I was gazing through gauzy curtains into the den, where the health-conscious Angela was furiously sweatin' to the oldies. So I rapped on the window to give her a chuckle, which must have startled her a bit because the springy steel exercise contraption she uses to firm up her pecs slipped her grip and came at me like a round from a bazooka, blowing the window glass to smithereens.

What followed was bedlam. Helicopters! Floodlights! Billy clubs! Choke holds! Lousy Neighborhood Watch weasels had dropped a dime on me! I had cops all over me, asking my name, demanding identification. As if I'd carry a wallet while burglarizing my own house. I mean, I'd have to be an idiot. . . .

Then Ange came out, looked me in the eyes, and told the fuzz to get me out of her yard, that she'd never laid eyes on me before.

That was nearly twelve hours ago. All night, Ange let me languish. And when she finally showed, she had a stranger with her, a stoop-shouldered guy in Hush Puppies and nubbly tweeds. He had very thick glasses with trendy round frames, which magnified his dark brown eyes and made him look simultaneously caring and startled. His hands were small and smooth. He didn't look handy at all. And even though I had a pretty good hunch who he might have been, I found myself liking him on impulse.

"Vincent," said Angie, "meet Dr. Nicholas Ruffalfalo." The doc stepped up to the cell and shook my hand through the bars. I smiled amiably at the two of them, then fell back on my cot.

"Nice try, Ange," I said, "but I keep telling you, therapy's not for me. Ain't going, no way, no how. And you," I muttered, pointing at the shrink, "just leave my mother out of this."

"You know, Vinnie," he replied, "it's normal to have anxieties about therapy, but it's just another kind of conversation."

"Doc, there's nothing here to sink your teeth into," I said. "I'm just a basic, regular guy. No kinks. No quirks. No craziness . . ."

"He says through the bars of his cell," cracked Ange. So I made a sourpuss face at Ange to let her know I wasn't going to budge.

"Fine," she said as she pulled a fistful of bail money from her purse and waved it in my face, "then I guess we won't be needing this."

"What do you mean?"

"Simple," she said. "Either you promise to meet with Dr. Ruffalfalo, or I'll let you rot in this dump."

I chortled. "You think that scares me? I can do this stretch standing on my head."

Just then a burly prison matron in shiny jack boots and crisp paramilitary togs tossed me a shrink-wrapped sandwich of gray egg salad on dried-out rye. "*Bon appetite,* Putz!" she grumbled, in passing.

"Hey, Burt," I called out cheerily. "Who was that, sweet old Aunt Bea?"

"Yep," Burt answered, appearing out of nowhere. "And here's the friendly town drunk, Otis."

Then my cell door swung open and Burt tossed in a glassy-eyed drifter type with a big brass nose ring and a bristly Mohawk coif. He was wearing leather bracelets, with spiky steel studs, and had a row of squiggly little swastikas amateurishly tattooed across his brow.

When I nodded hello, he flicked his tongue like a lizard and bugged out his eyes. "Redrum," he croaked in a raspy falsetto. "Redrum. Redd-rum."

"Well, okay then," said Ange, turning to leave. "You boys play nice."

I smiled broadly at the puzzled-looking shrink. "Why don't you pencil me in for next Tuesday morning?" I said. "Nine-ish good for you?"

10
Dr. Nick

Tuesday morning dawned bright and crisp and clear, and I was up early, prepping for my first visit to Nicholas J. Ruffalfalo, Ph.D., my soon-to-be soul mate, my consigliere-in-the-making, my highly educated spirit guide into the wide, wondrous Mystery of Me.

"Don't be nervous, Babe," I told Ange as she plucked cat fur from my lapel, "I've decided to push aside my misgivings and plunge into this therapy thing like an otter diving for a clam."

"Just be yourself," Ange answered, trying to hide the jitters in her voice. "Do you remember everything I told you?"

"Be honest?" I replied.

"Good. What else?"

"Be vulnerable?"

"Yep. What else?"

"No arm wrestling."

"Vincent . . ."

"Uhhhhh . . . No pig Latin? No yodeling?"

"Don't push me. . . ."

"I'm sorry, Ange. I can't remember the other thing you said."

"It's the most important thing."

"I'm drawing a blank," I said.

Ange grabbed the knot of my tie and yanked my face forward. "Listen very carefully," she said in firm, deliberate tones. "Don't try to fix anything!"

"Oh, yeah!" I laughed. "Of course I won't. Unless I spot some unsafe condition—"

"No!" she yelped. "You fix nothing, understand? Leave his office alone. I mean it. Screw this up and you'll spend more time in the basement than that pink aluminum Christmas tree you brought home seven years ago."

So adamant was Ange on this point, in fact, that I thought she might frisk me for concealed hand tools.

"Relax, Babe," I said. "I'll be a model patient." Then I kissed her good-bye, and raced off to my meeting with Dr. Nick.

Nick's office was situated in his home, a cozy bungalow on a nice lawn in a pleasant residential neighborhood. He met me in the tiny waiting room, and led me inside.

Somber diplomas and calming seascapes decked the sedate beige walls of the office. Nick offered me a seat in a plump leather swivel chair, then took his place in another. We sat quietly for a few moments as Nick seemed to size me up in a patient, friendly way, smiling, waiting for me to break the ice. So I decided to take the lead.

"I've never been to a therapist before," I told him as I opened the duffel bag at my feet, "and I wasn't sure of the protocol. So, just to be sure, I brought us a light midmorning snack."

I pulled Tupperware containers from the duffel and arranged them on the floor. "Okay," I said, "I brought baked ziti. Some ravioli stuffed with pesto gorgonzola. Here's nice gnocchi Bolognese. This is manicotti over here—three cheeses, I used. You like calzone? Made it myself. How about some fried polenta in marinara? A little salad? Some bread. Here's a nice little Barolo. You got a corkscrew?"

Nick seemed puzzled by my gesture of gustatory goodwill. "This is very generous, Vinnie," he said, "but generally, people don't eat during therapy."

"Really?"

Nick shook his head sagely. "They're discussing difficult things," he told me. "They're often confused and depressed. They're sometimes in despair. Most people don't think of food in such situations."

"That's one approach," I said. "Here's another." I handed him a silver serving spoon with a passage engraved in Italian, along the handle: *La vita è difficile con molto disappunto. Allora, mangiamo!*

"What does it mean?" asked Nick.

"It's the Agita family motto," I answered. "Roughly translated, it means 'Life is miserable and full of disappointment. Let's eat!'"

"That's very . . . wise," Nick muttered as he scribbled in the notebook on his lap. "But now, let's talk about you and Angela. As you know, I've spoken with her previously. She feels there are serious problems in your marriage."

"Here's one," I mumbled as I munched on the ziti. "I'm going blind like a cave fish from spending all my time in the cellar."

"She makes you live in the cellar?" he asked as I deftly slipped him a plate of the gnocchi.

I shook my head. "Mostly, I just have to sleep there."

"Booted from the bedroom, huh?"

"Dagwood Bumstead," I mumbled, "I feel your pain."

Nick chuckled politely. "Isn't there somewhere else you could sleep?" he asked.

"I could sleep in the den," I explained, "but that's Alphonse's sofa."

"Alphonse?"

"My cat," I said as I sampled the calzone.

"Couldn't Alphonse sleep in the basement?" asked Nick.

"No can do, Doc," I replied as Nick accepted a heaping plate of gnocchi. "Disturbing Alphonse would ruin one of the great joys of my life: I'm never more at peace than when my buddy Al is lost in the bottomless bliss of feline slumber."

"Peace? Bliss?" said Nick, sticking his fork in the pasta.

"Love watching that cat doze."

"Is that what you're after, Vincent? Solace?"

"Yeah, maybe," I said as I chomped on some crusty Tuscan bread. "Or maybe I just envy that cat's genius for logging high-quality sack time."

"You don't sleep well?"

"Can't turn off the mental turbines," I mumbled with my mouth full. "Brain keeps buzzing like a hive."

"What do you think about while you're lying there in bed?" asked Nick.

"The usual stuff," I replied as I passed him a provolone sandwich.

"Such as?"

"You know. Worries. Cares of the day."

"Give me an example."

"It's nothing, really . . ."

"Humor me," he insisted.

I set down my fork and gathered my thoughts. "Maybe I'll worry that the nose cone of a plummeting 747 is about to come smashing through my ceiling; maybe a lurking sinkhole is about to open up and swallow my house like a bullfrog snapping up a fly; perhaps deep inside the walls, all my electrical connections are all smoldering and sparking. That a lethal fog of radon, carbon monoxide, and methane fumes is seeping ever closer to the bedroom door. Or that somewhere out there in the rumbling heavens a gathering thunderbolt has already drawn a marksman's bead on my unsuspecting chimney. . . ."

Nick nodded as he set down his plate and wiped his chin. He'd heard enough. "I'm sensing a deep mistrust in the goodness of the universe," he said with compassion and concern. "Now, yes, it's true; bad things happen to good people," he counseled, "but you have to have faith in the goodness of life. The world is not always a hostile place, Vincent. Calamity does not lurk at every corner. Disaster is not always on the rise."

I licked some sauce from the back of my spoon. "Did Ange tell you I've been struck by lightning seventeen times?" I asked.

"Seventeen times?" he snapped.

"Twelve times when I was testing the Zeuss-Master Z2000."

"The what?"

"My prototype for a personal, backpack-mounted lightning rod system," I explained. "If I perfect this baby, you could play golf right through the most violent thunderstorms—take a few thousand volts on the backswing, channel it all into your drive."

"Some bugs in the prototype, I'm guessing," said Nick, showing signs of being a quick learner.

"Melted my Weejuns to the bluegrass," I confessed. "But the ball carried, like, to Venus."

"And the other five times were random strikes?" Nick asked as he set aside his gnocchi and accepted a plate of olives and cheese.

"Bolts from the blue," I confirmed.

Nick chewed thoughtfully on a tangy Calamata. "How do you explain this?" he asked.

I shrugged as I sliced the onion-and-herb frittata. Nick stroked his chin for a moment, then shifted in his chair. "Let's try a different tack for a moment," he said. "Tell me about your dreams. Any particularly troubling or frustrating ones come to mind?"

I nodded eagerly as I munched. "Here's a good one," I told him. "Had it last night: I come home, it's pouring, my arms are full of groceries. I manage to turn the key in the lock, but when I shoulder the door, it doesn't budge. The humidity has caused it to swell, and it's jammed solid in the frame. I call for Ange, but she can't hear me. So I'm trapped out on the stoop, getting soaked to my skin."

Nick seemed interested. "What might this jammed door be keeping you from?" he asked.

"From entering my house," I answered.

"And how does that make you feel?"

"Like I can't get into my house," I explained.

"Expand on that for me."

"Like I'm stuck outside my house."

"Go deeper," he implored.

"Like there's no way to get into my house," I said.

Nick gave me a coaxing wave, and I began to

sweat as I struggled to give him what he wanted. "Like I won't be going in there," I offered. "Like I'm getting very wet. Like if someone asked the question, Where in the world can you *not* go? I would be able to point at my house and say, among other places, definitely, *in there.*"

Nick blew out a loud sigh and gazed out the window.

"There are some powerful images here," he said. "Symbols of longing and emotional frustration. You want to enter your home—a symbol of security and wholeness. You have emotional gifts to give—the groceries. You call to your wife, but she can't hear you—a vivid depiction of isolation. And you see, by peering through the window, all the warmth and love and security you crave. But the jammed door thwarts you. It's a very poignant metaphor."

Nick paused momentarily and gazed thoughtfully at the ceiling. "My point is this," he continued. "I suspect this dream is connected, in some obscure and mysterious way, to the deep, emotional source of your troubles with Angela."

"Or maybe," I suggested as I screwed the lid off the Thermos, "it's connected to what happened to me yesterday afternoon."

"What was that?"

"I came home from the supermarket with my arms full of groceries, the door was jammed, and I got stuck in the pouring rain." I offered Nick a demitasse. "Espresso?" I said.

Nick slumped back in his chair. I offered him a plate of coffee-and-almond cookies. He waved them off absently, and kept staring at me in wonder and sympathy, like I was one of those poor little calves with two heads. Five minutes he sat, without saying a word. Some subtle new form of therapy, I figured.

11
Young, Handy, and in Love

"How would you like to start today?" I asked my therapist, Nick, at the beginning of our second session. "Maybe some word association? You say *tomato,* I say *to-mah-to;* you say *potato,* and I say I think I'm Napoleon. . . ."

Nick's frown showed he was not amused. "I'd rather hear a little about your childhood," he said.

"I was a regular kid," I said, with an accompanying shrug. "Handier than most, maybe, and that led to some problems."

"What kind of problems?" Nick inquired.

"The other kids didn't understand my handy urges," I explained. "I mean, I didn't play stickball, I didn't play hoops. I was happier shingling a roof or snaking out a drain. So, mostly they shunned me. They called me Chisel-Face, Tool-Weirdo, Plunger-Boy. Once in a while, if they caught me working on a toilet, they'd treat me to a quick, bracing swirly."

"Kids can be so cruel," said Nick.

"Especially the unhandy ones," I replied.

"You told me Angela lived on your street," Nick recalled. "Do you think she thought you were weird?"

"At first, probably," I said, "but then she got to know me."

"You never told me how you and Angela met," Nick pointed out.

"It's a long story," I said, "but I can tell you, handiness played a pivotal role."

Nick leaned back in his swivel chair and laid his notebook on his knees. "Let's get started," he said. "I think I need to hear this."

The saga begins on a sweltering August day many years ago when I, little Vinnie Agita, was a precocious handy maverick only nine years old. I was sitting on the curb outside my family's row house, dabbing with a Popsicle stick at the molten asphalt between my feet, pretending it was roofing tar I was spreading on a leaky flat roof.

All around me, the street was full of summer bustle. Neighbors fanned themselves and chattered on their stoops; at the corner, a bunch of boys were struggling to wrench open the spray valve of a hydrant, and across the street, sitting on the opposite curb, was Angela Narducci, the most beautiful nine-year-old girl in the world, who was holding in her arms what might have been the homeliest kitten in the county. Don't get me wrong, I love animals, but this was one plug-ugly kitty: Her eyes were crossed, most of her right ear was missing, and, thanks to a congenital deformation of the upper lip, she looked like she was always about to yodel.

Angie didn't care. She had rescued the kitten from the alley, clipped the mats from its fur, fed it, named it Petunia, and convinced her mother to let her bring it home. Other kids teased her about her goofy-looking pet, but Angie just ignored them. She loved that homely cat completely—which was, to me, just one more bit of proof that Angie was entirely perfect.

Of course, I loved her madly and would have told her so if I didn't go apoplectic every time she came near me. One single glance from her and I melted. I wheezed. I stammered and trembled. I blushed like a freshly poached salmon. It was mortifying. So I kept a respectful distance and resigned myself to a lifetime of loving her hopelessly from afar.

There came a whoop of jubilation from the boys at the corner when they finally freed the frozen hydrant valve, and a plume of city water geysered two stories high. No one noticed as the boys frolicked in the street that the runoff from the hydrant had flash flooded the gutter and was raging, in the shape of a miniature tsunami, along the curb where Angie and Petunia were playing.

The timing was horrific: Petunia gave Angie a play bite on the arm and leapt rebelliously down off her lap just as the raging torrent reached them and swept the kitten away. Angie's red Keds splashed in the gutter as she desperately raced to save her pet, but the flow was too swift, and in an instant, Petunia had been whisked down the mouth of a sewer.

"Petunia!" howled Angie. "Somebody save her!" Her screams brought people running, but no one knew what to do. It was awful. The sewer mouth was just a narrow slash cut under the curb. You couldn't even stick your head in there to look down into the shaft. Angie just kept screaming. Then she spotted me sitting on the curb. Our eyes locked. She looked into my soul. "Save her!" she cried. I felt all the blood drain down into my sneakers. Angie just kept staring, like everything was up to me.

I don't know how I made my way to my father's workshop. I don't remember what I was thinking as I rummaged through the bins and shelves and drawers. But in minutes, I'd gathered a puzzling pile of junk on my father's workbench. There were pulleys, gears, fishing line, sprockets, wire, switches, hinges, and spools; I tossed in a roll of duct tape, lead solder, Lincoln Logs, some random parts from my Erector set, and the motor from my mother's old Hoover.

What was my plan? I had none. I was following blind handy instinct. I don't know how long I labored under that magical handy spell, but when I was finished, I'd created something wondrous and odd.

It looked like a miniature offshore oil rig bolted to a plywood platform. There was a bare-bones superstructure of Erector-set trusses, several different boom arms with full-swivel capability, a D-cell battery for plenty of working power, and a panel of push buttons and joystick toggles that, with any luck, would control the contraption's functions without setting the whole damn thing on fire.

When I burst out of the house with my strange creation in my arms, the street was full of people. I fought my way through the crowd and placed the machine at the mouth of the sewer. People cackled derisively as I lay down on the street, but they gasped and fell silent when I punched a button and a sleek boom arm telescoped into the darkness of the sewer. Then I flipped a switch, and they oohed and ahhed as the miniature flashlight attached to the tip of the boom cast a small but brilliant spotlight on the slimy back wall of the sewer.

Next, I wiggled the joystick toggles, and watched—thanks to a system of carefully angled dental mirrors—as the articulating tip of the boom sent the flashlight beacon sweeping back and forth inside the sewer. At first, there was nothing down there but the bubbling swirl of the water draining down into the sewer system.

Then I saw a faint green glimmer: cat's eyes! It was Petunia. She was bobbing in the drink, and paddling frantically against the downward tug of the sewer.

There was no time to waste. I flipped a second toggle, and a spool whirled, feeding out fishing line to lower a small toy scoop shovel, stolen from an old Tonka truck. Working the controls wildly, I let the scoop shovel snap at the water. Petunia went under once, twice; I missed the mark again and again. Then the black swirl sucked her down for good. I closed my eyes, said a prayer to all that is merciful and handy, and let the scoop shovel fall one last time. My heart leapt as I felt a squirming weight on the end of the line.

"Got her!" I cried.

"Petunia!" screamed Angie.

Angie was sobbing with joy as I winched the soggy cat back up to daylight. The crowd let out a cheer. Angela's mother was waiting with a towel, and they wrapped Petunia up and took her home. Then the crowd thinned—it was almost dinnertime—and I was left alone to savor my moment of glory. For a while, I sat on the curb, replaying the drama in my mind. I imagined what people must be thinking: "Thank God that Vinnie kid dreamed up that contraption. There's no other way anyone could have gotten to the cat."

It was true. Nobody could have wriggled into that sewer. The opening was definitely narrower than a human head. I eyeballed it. No way a head fits in there. I was sure of it. Fairly certain anyway. Pretty damn convinced. Oh, what the hell, only one way to know for sure.

So I lay down in the street and tried to slide my head through the drain opening. Sure enough, it pressed tight against my temples. Impossible to get a head in there, even if you pushed really hard, like *this*.

And that's how I found out my head indeed could fit, just barely, through that very narrow drain. Almost instantly, I made a related discovery: Just because a head slides into a tight space, doesn't necessarily mean the same exact head will just slide right back out.

And just like that, *Mama mia!* My head was trapped in the sewer.

But before I had time to panic, I felt a presence behind me. Straining my gaze sideways, I saw a pair of sopping wet, bright red Keds.

"What're you doing?" asked Angie.

I had to think fast. "Inspecting the sewer," I replied.

"Why?"

"I'm looking for ways we can make this safer," I said, "so no other kittens fall in."

Angie thought it over. "Your head's stuck, isn't it?" she said.

"My head isn't stuck." I chuckled, but the desperation in my laughter echoed back to me from within the smelly hollow shaft.

"Then why don't you come out?"

"I told you."

"You're inspecting."

VINCE RAUSE

"Right." I couldn't believe my first real conversation with the woman I loved was happening while my head was stuck in a sewer.

"I just wanted to tell you thanks for saving Petunia," said Ange.

"Okay," I sheepishly replied.

"It was really nice," she said.

I reached an arm behind my head and managed a backward wave. There was an uncomfortable silence. Then Angie bent way down and sideways so I could see her face. "Kids think you're weird," she said, her hair dangling in the wet gutter. "But I think you're, like, a hero."

Then she sat on the curb above me and waited for the firemen to come and jackhammer me free. We didn't say a word.

It seemed that to speak would shatter the spell, so we just sat there in magical silence. Everything seemed so right, you know? But alas, the magic did not last. Once they had me out of the oddly comforting confines of the sewer, all my Ange-related anxieties returned. I convinced myself that she was just being nice out of gratitude, and I didn't want to do anything stupid that might ruin the most perfect moment of my life. So I decided to avoid her, and I did so for months. Then, later that fall, her father, Fiore, a florist who dabbled in commodities, hit it big in provolone futures and moved the family out to the distant burbs.

I never stopped loving her, of course, though I never expected to see her again. But the handy fates

112

had other plans, and ten years later, when I was nine-teen years old, I crossed paths once again with Angela Narducci. Fittingly, it was plumbing, the most poetic of all handy arts, that finally brought us together.

It was the summer after high school. I was trying to scrape together tuition for community college that fall, and my Uncle Sal, a master plumber, was throwing some work my way when he could. It was in August, I think, he got a call from Fiore Narducci, Angie's dad, to come out to their sprawling suburban split-level and remodel the master bath. It was a good week's wages, so I was happy to help, but I was nervous about seeing Ange.

As it turned out, Ange was off attending summer semester at her swanky New England girls' school and wasn't due home for a week. Sal and I would be long gone by then. Still, it was weird being in her house. There were photos of her everywhere—she had grown into a dark-eyed, willowy beauty, big surprise—and her stuff was still scattered all over: the books she loved, the records she listened to, old bottles of leftover perfume, and God help me, the very bed she slept in.

It was haunting, working in that house and bathing in her aura, and it began to work on me in odd and unsettling ways. My appetite faded. I dreamed of her every night. I grew sullen and listless, and I don't have to tell you, my plumbing skills slid straight to hell. It didn't take Uncle Sal very long to notice.

"Hand me the spud wrench," he barked one day as

he lay on his broad back, with his bulky torso wedged into the narrow cabinet beneath the new sink. I sluggishly obliged. Sally grumbled and dragged himself out into the open.

"What's this?" he said, waggling a peppers-and-egg hero in my mug.

"Sorry," I muttered as I handed him the spud wrench.

He tossed me the sandwich. "You didn't eat your lunch again?"

"I'm not very hungry today."

"You weren't hungry yesterday," said Sally.

"Maybe I'm getting a twenty-four-hour bug," I replied.

"Maybe you're getting permanently stupid," he said. "I ask for a wrench, you hand me a sandwich. I tell you to solder a pipe, you set the wall on fire. And yesterday, I found that Timex Twist-O-Flex I gave you for graduation welded to the P trap under the sink."

"I have a lot on my mind," I said as I glanced at my wrist, which, amazingly, was naked.

"I know what you got on your mind," he said as he leaned back against the vanity. "It's Fiore's daughter. I see you mooning over her picture. I see you peeking in her room. Admit it, you're crazy about her and you don't know what to do."

Sally had me nailed, and there was no use staging a denial. "What can I do?" I griped. "A girl like that, she wouldn't look at me twice."

"How do you know until you try?"

I looked away with a shrug and accidentally saw myself reflected in the mirrored doors of the shower. My face was smudged with grease and plumber's putty. I was wearing baggy, borrowed overalls that drooped comically in the butt and sported a name patch with "Bo-Bo" embroidered on a field of white, and on my head was a ball cap with my uncle's company logo—a flying cartoon plunger with pudgy Cupid wings—emblazoned on the peak.

"Trust me," I said to Sal, "I have a pretty good hunch on this one."

Sally waved a crescent wrench in my face. "Listen to me," he said. "If you live your life afraid to take a risk, your old age will be filled with regrets. Ask the girl out. The worst she can say is no. Just give her a present. How hard is that?"

"What kind of present?" I asked.

"Something unique," he said. "Something no one else can give her."

I thought it over. Sal was right.

"I'm going to make her something," I said.

"Attaboy," said Sally, squeezing my arm in approval, "but promise me, nothing that might catch fire."

We finished up on a Friday morning, and Uncle Sal was anxious to close out the job. "Bingo!" he cried as he gave the sleek chrome faucets a final loving polish. "I'll go settle with Fiore; you gather up the tools and meet me in the truck."

As Sal clomped down the stairs, I reached into my

pocket and pulled out a small black-velvet pouch. Carefully, I opened the pouch and looked at the trinket inside. It was a pendant, in the shape of a dozing, one-eared cat. I cast it myself from molten plumber's solder, and power buffed it until it gleamed like sterling silver.

On the back, I had engraved a poem of my own composition. I'd been up all night trying to capture my thoughts on paper, but the words and rhymes failed me until finally, at dawn, I threw in the towel. But as I bent over the sink bowl to wash my face I was granted inspiration, and the words came to me in a flash:

> *My love, as pure and endless as the waters*
> *Which from these glistening fixtures rush,*
> *Will speak my name each time you bathe,*
> *And every time you flush.*

It was music. It was perfect. It was me. So I scratched the lines into the back of the pendant with a six-penny nail, and that was that.

Now, my plan was to sneak into Angie's bedroom and slip the box beneath her pillow. Ange was due home the following morning. She would find the pouch when she went to bed, and *que sera, sera.*

But before I could make my move, I heard a car door slam in the driveway. I stepped to the window and saw a slender, tanned brunette stepping from a cab. She was wearing enormous sunglasses. A backpack was slung over her shoulder, and in her right hand she carried a small wire cage containing a cat.

"Ange!" cried Fiore as he burst from the house and hugged his daughter. "You're home early!"

The pictures hadn't done her justice. She was breathtaking. When she hugged her burly father and the sun hit her upturned face, all the strength drained from my body. My tongue swelled. My heart thumped. I felt like a clumsy kid again, in full-blown Ange-inspired panic. I glanced at the worthless trinket in my hand. What was I thinking?

My uncle bellowed up the stairs, "Let's go, Vincent! Move move move!"

"Coming!" I answered as I hurried to stuff the pendant back into the pouch. But in my haste I fumbled it and watched with dismay as it hit the top of the toilet tank and bounced behind the john.

"Vincent!" roared Uncle Sal. "Now! Let's go!"

"On my way," I answered as I fell to my belly and began to wiggle behind the toilet. It was a tight squeeze, but I strained forward until I could see the trinket wedged behind the tank. I had to arch my back to reach it, and when I did, I felt an intense cranial pressure. I realized with a sinking sense of doom that my head was now wedged like a nut in a cracker, between the toilet bowl and the adjacent wall.

"Don't panic," I told myself, "make a plan." But the only plan I could think of was to thrash like a netted tuna, which only wedged my head more tightly. When I paused to catch my breath, I felt a quiet presence behind me.

Angela.

"Are you all right?" she said.

Oh please . . .

"I'm fine," I cheerily responded.

"You're head's stuck, isn't it?" she said.

"No," I chuckled, "I'm just making one last check on some connections back here. . . ."

Ange was quiet for a moment. Then she leaned forward, trying to get a better look at my head.

"Do I know you?" she asked.

"I'm really trying to concentrate down here," I snapped.

But Ange wouldn't have it. The next thing I knew, she had grabbed my baggy overalls in her fists, and was grunting and tugging like a dock worker. My head was jammed tighter than a champagne cork, but Angie was no quitter, and with one last furious heave, she gave a mighty tug and pulled me free. Ange fell back on her can; I ended up on her lap. Reaching forward, she grabbed my chin and jerked my head around so she could look into my kisser.

"I knew it," she said. "It's you. Vinnie."

Mortified, I scrambled to my feet and began gathering my uncle's tools.

"How have you been?" she asked as she rose from the floor. "It's been a long time."

I couldn't answer. My throat felt like sandpaper. My heart was beating so hard, I swear, the pencils in my pocket protector were doing the Wave. God, she was so beautiful in person. But all I wanted was to be out of there, pronto.

"So, you're a plumber now?" she said as I hoisted Uncle Sal's toolbox and headed for the door.

"I gotta go load these tools," I mumbled.

Ange clucked her tongue at me and said, "Aren't you even going to say hello?"

I flopped my arms apologetically and explained, "My uncle's waiting in the truck."

"I won't keep you," she said with a chilly smile. "Just let me ask you—why wouldn't you talk to me?"

"Excuse me?"

"When we were kids. I mean, you do this wonderful thing for me, you save my cat, you save me from the worst heartbreak I could imagine, and the next day you cross the street when you see me coming. You never speak to me again."

The muscles in my chest were tightening now, and I had to concentrate just to breathe. I managed an awkward grin, then I realized she was waiting for an answer.

"Sorry," I said, "I didn't mean anything by it."

Ange nodded. Actually it was more like a series of rapid head twitches. I have since learned to recognize and respect this warning sign, but back then I didn't know her, so I never saw it coming when she grabbed my lapels and slammed me back against the wall.

"Didn't mean anything?" she shouted. "Didn't mean anything? Well, here's what it meant to me, Bub! It meant I had a real live hero when I was nine years old, but he wouldn't talk to me. So I've been looking for another one ever since. And that's a problem, see, because every time I meet a boy I like, I expect him to be odd and amazing. I expect him to be sweet and weird and brave. But things never work out, because as soon as I start to care about a boy, I can't help it—I picture him with his head stuck in a sewer. And they never look good in that picture; they just look like a bunch of poor dumb yutzes with their heads stuck in a sewer."

Suddenly Ange stopped talking. Her eyes were shining with rage. I was certain she was going to slug me. Then a chubby one-eared cat sauntered into the room, strolled directly to the toilet, crouched beneath the tank, and with some quick, deft paw work, plucked the pendant free.

"Petunia," said Angie as the pendant hit the floor, "what is that?"

As if on cue, Petunia slapped the pendant across the floor like a tavernkeeper sliding a brewski down the bartop. Angie was very quiet as she studied the pendant. She turned it over several times. Finally she smiled and bounced it on her palm. "Now this," she said, "is amazing. And very, very weird."

Then, as Petunia held us in her cross-eyed gaze, Angie kissed me, and as simply as that, our life of love and handiness had begun.

12
Bizarro Vinnie

ast night, I dreamed I was a handyman on the planet Bizarro. You know Bizarro, don't you? It's that wacky, backward world so vividly documented in the Superman comics.

On Bizarro, every facet of life is flipped upside down: People say "Good-bye" when they answer the phone; they wear their suits to bed and go to work in their pajamas; Bizarro cats are afraid of mice and Bizarro dogs bark "Wow-wow-bow!"

But to me, the most remarkable thing is that on this looney cartoon planet, the primary job of the handyman is to break things, a freakish irony that turns the very essence of handiness on its ear. Consider, for example, that the Bizarro Maytag repairman is the busiest guy in town. His phone never stops ringing. "You gotta get over here," his exasperated customers plead. "My washer's working perfectly!"

Of course, the astute reader might point out that on Bizarro, Maytag washers would be pieces of junk, so everyone would love them and the repair guy would still be bored and lonely. But one might also theorize that to the average Bizarran, boredom and loneliness are feelings to be craved.

One might spend hours, in fact, chasing the endless, loopy spiral of Bizarro logic until one would need a fistful of Advil and a stiff belt of Scotch. (Unless, of course, one was a Bizarran, in which case a nice tension headache might be a very special treat, indeed.)

You see what I mean. Anyway, here's what's bothering me: In the dream, I was on *Oprah,* and she asked me to reveal my favorite handyman tips. I wracked my Bizarro brain and came up with the following:

1. To avoid the dangers of frostbite, shovel snow only in the summer months.

2. In a pinch, an unexploded shell from a past world war makes an excellent mallet for pile-driving posts or tenderizing meat.

3. Before operating heavy machinery, be sure to down five or six really potent cold pills with a quick martini chaser.

Well, I woke in a cold sweat and bolted from the bed, horrified to the center of my handy being, to know that such disturbing thoughts were rumbling around down in my subconscious. So I made an emergency appointment with Nick, my shrink. Nick had never heard of Bizarro, so I had to bring him up to speed.

"Everything's backward there," I said. "People use umbrellas only when the sun shines, they brush their teeth *before* all meals, and on Bizarro, everybody thinks O.J. is guilty."

"Most people think that here," said Nick.

"I know," I said. "It's the one thing that carries over."

Nick nodded sagely. "So the dream has upset you?"

"It rattled me good," I replied. "What do you think it means?"

Nick shrugged reflectively. "Dreams are often telling us things we already know but are afraid to face," he counseled.

"You mean, the dream's telling me I'm a lousy handyman?"

"Only you can interpret the meaning of the dream," said Nick. "You have to ask yourself, How did it make me feel?"

I mulled it over. "Somehow, it made me feel devious," I said.

"Devious?" Nick replied.

"Devious, and petty," I replied.

Nick settled back in his chair. "I don't get devious and petty from that dream," he admitted.

"That's because you don't know what I know," I confessed. Then the floodgates broke, and I owned up to the handy shame inside me.

"I'm a small, stingy person, Doc," I sobbed. "People depend on me for handy guidance, and I've been holding out on them."

"I don't follow," said Nick. "You give me handy guidance all the time, even though I never ask."

I nodded, trying to stifle the tears. "Sure, I pass along a tip or two, but I never give up the good stuff. The blue chip tips. The real precious gems of handy insider know-how. No, those glorious bits I keep to myself. Even though they came to me freely—from TV shows, or how-to books, or the selfless generosity of fellow handy scholars—I did not pass them along, as the handyman code compels me; instead I have selfishly squirreled them away in my head, like a miser hoarding his pennies. Oh, the arrogance! The pride! I wanted that knowledge all to myself! I wanted to feel smarter—handier—than the rest."

Nick sat silently for a while. "I've never actually dealt with this particular problem before," he candidly confessed. "But it seems to be causing you a lot of guilt. So it seems to me you can either live with the guilt, or find a way to set things right."

"That's what I want," I said. "I want to set things right."

"Then, share the tips," he advised.

And that's exactly what I did—I went straight home and composed a list of ten common handy problems, and the inspired handyman tips that make them easy to solve. I now present this list to you, for your handy edification, with sincere apologies for welshing on you all this time.

Problem 1. Whenever you move your stepladder, a bruising cascade of hammers, pry bars, chisels, and other items made of case-hardened steel rains down upon your head from the ladder's top step, where you'd forgotten you'd left them. Despite the pretty flash of white-hot light, and the bright swirling colors, you are worried that in the long run, this could land you in a sheltered workshop setting.

Vinnie Tip 1. Fasten a small plastic storage tub to the ladder's top step with a few short drywall screws, and you have yourself a built-in tool tray. Takes just a minute, and it sure beats lengthy head trauma rehab.

Problem 2. Your showerhead is crusted over with hard-water deposits, and the little spray holes are all plugged up so that all you get when you turn on the faucet is some pathetically anemic crosswise spritzing.

Vinnie Tip 2. Unscrew the showerhead and boil it in a pan of vinegar. Acids in the vinegar will dissolve the deposits, and the showerhead will once again spray like new.

Problem 3. You need to drive a tiny nail in a tight corner, but the nail always slips before you get it started, and you keep waffling your thumbnail with the hammer.

Vinnie Tip 3. Slip the nail between the teeth of a plastic comb, or a slit in a piece of cardboard, and use the comb to hold the nail in place while you tap the nail head lightly to get it started. *(Note:* Please make sure your comb is nail-free come styling time; in any case, don't come whining to me because some overlooked carpet tack has ruined your precious hair-replacement system.)

Problem 4. Your showerhead and the pipe it's attached to (the "shower arm") shudder when the water's turned on and wobble unpleasantly when you touch them. You find this situation so unsettling that your personal hygiene is at risk.

Vinnie Tip 4. Shower pipes wobble when the metal straps securing them to the wall studs loosen. If you can get to the pipes through an access panel in the wall, replacing these straps is as simple as driving a few nails. If there's no easy access, don't worry about chopping into the plaster. Just loosen the shower arm's trim plate, which will reveal the hole in the wall through which the shower pipe passes. Now get yourself a can of aerosol insulating foam and spray it through the hole. This stuff expands dramatically and hardens as it dries. Just tape the shower arm in the correct position. The foam will surround your pipes as it fills the wall cavity between the studs and firmly lock your shower's plumbing in place.

Problem 5. You spend big bucks on expensive caulking in those cardboard tubes, use only a dollop or two, and sit by helplessly as the rest promptly hardens into a useless rubbery mass because the tube's little plastic nozzle is so hard to seal.

Vinnie Tip 5. "Wire nuts"—the colorful plastic twist-on caps used to make electrical connections—will give your caulking tubes an airtight seal when twisted on over those soft plastic nozzles. Buy a few different sizes to make sure you get one that fits.

Problem 6. Your old metal framing square with which you have fought many a handy battle has darkened and corroded over the years, until the numbered measurements stamped along the ruled edge are indecipherable. You fear the time has come to say good-bye.

Vinnie Tip 6. You can revive old metal measuring tools by smearing on, then wiping off, a coat of white paint. The paint remains in the stamped markings, making them highly visible once again.

Problem 7. You want to spray paint, say, some small wooden drawer knobs for a kid's desk. You hate the idea of those nasty spray-paint fumes drifting through your house, but it's too breezy outside to do the job in the open air.

Vinnie Tip 7. You can make a miniature outdoor spray-paint booth by simply turning a cardboard box on its side. Put whatever you want to paint inside the box and spray away. The sides of the box will block the wind, and you won't have to worry about overspray.

Problem 8. Don't you hate it when you're drilling in the ceiling, and the little crumbs of plaster or drywall keep falling in your eye? Even if you're wearing goggles, and you should be, bits of crumble rubble fall all over the floor. Then you step down and grind them into the hardwood, or smash them into the weave of an heirloom rug. I don't know about your house, but at my place, this has earned me, more than once, an unrequested weekend getaway to the basement couch.

Vinnie Tip 8. Before drilling into the ceiling, push your drill bit through the center of an old pie plate. Hold the pie plate steady, run the drill, and let the pan catch the fallout.

Problem 9. In preparation for painting the dining room trim, you carefully masked off all edges with tape, hoping to get sharp, clean lines. But when the paint dried and you pulled off the tape, you pulled off patches of the new paint too. Now you need to sand all those ragged patches, and paint all over again.

Vinnie Tip 9. Before removing masking tape from a freshly painted surface, warm the tape gently with a hair dryer. The dryer's heat will loosen the tape's grip, and allow you to safely peel it away.

Problem 10. The last time you rearranged the wall hangings in your bedroom, you were stunned to see that the wallpaper was scarred beyond belief by all the picture hangers you'd driven into the walls.

Vinnie Tip 10. Next time you hang a picture, use a razor knife to cut a neat triangular flap in the wallpaper, exposing the plaster at the point where you plan to drive your nail. Fold down the flap, and drive your nail into the uncovered plaster. When you remove the picture, dab a little wallpaper glue on the wall and carefully press the triangular flap back in place for an invisible repair.

When I finished my list, I felt reborn, forgiven. As usual, Nick's advice had carried me through. Although his suggestion that I discuss the Bizarro dream with Angie didn't pan out so nicely. It happened right after that session at Nick's. I came home, and told Angie all about the list I was going to write, and the dream that inspired it. She was completely confused because, like Nick, she'd never heard of the planet Bizarro.

"It's reverse reality," I said. "It's a place where I'd be the opposite of everything I am."

"You wouldn't be handy?" she asked.

"I'd probably have some cushy executive job," I answered. "Probably live in a swank condo. Drive a big honkin' Lexus. Have myself some nubile young trophy wife—"

They say that when you step on a land mine, you hear a little click, and then there's silence, and that is the signal that all is lost. But still, one wouldn't be a man if one didn't struggle.

"I should point out," I chuckled, "that I meant a Bizarro trophy wife, who would be the exact opposite of you—a very bad-looking trophy wife is what I meant, see, heh-heh, it's the total opposite of here."

Ange just nodded.

"Oh, heck," I said, "I see the problem. You just don't get the concept of Bizarro logic."

"Oh, I think I do," said Angie. "Like, for example, on the Bizarro planet, you'd be sleeping in your own cozy bed tonight."

Later that night, as I dozed off on the basement sofa, I began to dream I was back on the planet Bizarro.

Bizarro Vinnie had just swung around with a ladder and smashed a prized antique vase to smithereens.

"Oh, you've ruined my beautiful vase!" cried Bizarro Angela. "I'm going to bake you a pie! And then, I'm giving you a sponge bath."

What can I tell you? A guy's gotta dream.

13
Cracks

My shrink, Nick, asked how things were going, and I told him I had cracks. They're everywhere, I said, spidery little veins of shame. Implying weakness. Unwholesomeness. A shaky foundation. A trembling at the core.

"Something's shifting," I said. "Something fundamental."

"Tell me about these . . . cracks," said Nick, with an eager gleam in his eye. "For example, can anyone else see them?"

"I don't let anyone see them," I said. "I hide them from people. They make me ashamed."

"What, in particular, bothers you about these . . . cracks?" he asked.

"They're persistent," I answered. "You cover them

up and you think they're gone for good, but no, they come back, again and again. Why, Doc?" I implored. "Where do they come from?"

Nick's eyes widened with hope and amazement. "What do *you* think, Vincent?" he said. "What do you think is causing these cracks?"

I sucked in my breath and made myself say it: "I'm afraid," I said, "that my Lally post is failing."

Nick, who is handy-impaired, looked puzzled. "Your lollipop?" he said.

"My Lally post. It holds up the beam beneath the wall with all the cracks. I think I have some subsidence down there and it's wreaking havoc on my plaster."

Nick disappeared for a moment, then came back with a cold towel. He sat back in his swivel chair, draped the towel over his eyes and told me we were done for the day. "No charge," he said. "I just need to nap a little."

At first it shocked me that Nick took the news so hard, but then again, many people have strong reactions to the strange and mysterious phenomenon of cracking.

Cracks, by the way, happen because your house moves. It's moving all the time. It heaves and leans and sways. It shrinks and swells according to the weather. It does a regular rumba when a bus rolls by.

All this movement is minute, but still, it puts stress on your plaster, which, being brittle, tends to crack. Please be assured that most of the cracks in your walls are only the harmless result of the natural, gentle movements of your domicile. Except, of course, for the ones that mean the dump's about to crumble.

Hey, hey! Get out from under that table and pay attention. You have plenty of time. If you know what to look for, serious cracks will give you plenty of warning before the roof ends up in the rumpus room. Just this one proviso: If you have any cracks that are, say, an inch or so in width, grab the kids and the cat and a few precious momentos and get yourself out in the open right now. There may be a Red Cross cot in your immediate future.

So, how do we tell the harmless cracks from the scary deadly ones? First, we measure. Use a ruler marked off in sixty-fourths of an inch, and measure across the widest point.

Forget about cracks one-sixteenth of an inch or less in width; they're only a cosmetic problem and we'll show you how to patch them up next week. Start worrying, though, if you see cracks a quarter-inch wide or wider; these might be the signs of serious structural failure, that your house is being rendered limb from limb.

But not necessarily. A wide crack doesn't always mean disaster. What really matters is whether or not the crack is active. That is, does it continue to widen, indicating that whatever structural problem may have caused the crack is getting worse? Or, has it stabilized, meaning your worries may be over?

Let's find out by watching the crack for movement.

Such movement, of course, is excruciatingly slow—an active crack may widen maybe a millimeter or so in a six-month stretch. So get yourself a comfy chair and a Big Gulp with refills. Heh-heh-heh. Just kidding. No one would sit still that long, staring at a wall. Except maybe for those Hindu mystics who have complete mastery of all their desires. And then there are the people who like to watch golf on TV.

But here's a better way to monitor crack movement: Draw parallel pencil lines on either side of the crack, record the date and the width between the lines, then measure again at six-month intervals. If the distance increases, the next step is to calculate the speed of the movement. If the crack widens a little less in each six-month period, that means things are getting better and at some point the crack will stabilize, and then you can patch it.

If the crack is widening at an accelerating rate, however, it could mean that your house is very tired and would like to lie down for a while.

Chances are that whatever structural flaws are causing the cracks can be safely corrected, but first you have to find them. And that's where structural cracks can be downright handy, because, if you know how to read them, they'll point out your problem like the arrow of a compass.

For example, say you see diagonal cracks in a western wall of your house. These are "tension shear cracks," which happen when one part of a house pulls away from another. Tension cracks always rise, diagonally, toward the offending structural member. In this case, the cracks slope up toward the adjoining southern wall, so it's a good bet that the south wall is settling and pulling away, creating the stress that is causing the cracks.

Likewise, say you spot tension cracks on both walls of a bedroom corner, sloping up toward the corner itself, then find the same pattern in the dining room below. The cracks are pointing up to a post that, most likely, has rotted, allowing that corner of the house to slump. (Remember, tension shear cracks always rise up to point toward the problem.)

Okay, a whole new problem: You find, on an eastern wall, a pyramid pattern of diagonal cracks. You also spot some crumbling along the fissure. This kind of crack, a "compression shear" fracture, is a whole different kind of cat. Compression cracks are caused by one part of the house bearing down, with crushing weight, on another. And here's the tip-off: These cracks always slope *down* toward the problem.

In the case of the pyramid cracks mentioned above, we have one set of cracks pointing down at the adjoining south wall, and another set pointing down at the adjoining north wall. Get the picture? The north and south walls are settling, while the east wall, supported by a beefy steel column down in the basement, is standing pat. The sinking motion of the outside walls is tugging down on the ends of the east wall, bending it down over the sturdy post, like a strong man bending an iron bar over his knee. But plaster doesn't bend, hence, the telltale compression fractures.

What causes a house to sink and lean? In old houses, weak foundations are often the culprit. Rot, moisture, and the natural decay of wood and stone also play a role. But one of the most regrettable, and avoidable, causes of structural failure is—and it hurts me to admit it—misguided handy activity.

See, a house is designed to maintain a delicate balance, and anything that throws off that balance—which redirects loads in ways the house can't handle—can do structural harm.

Plumbers, electricians, and HVAC guys, for example, are often less than surgical when cutting access routes for their pipes, ducts, and wires. (In my own house, while gutting the kitchen ceiling, I uncovered, directly above the sink, two second-story floor joists that had been so savagely chopped to make way for new plastic pipes that in some places they were less than three inches thick. The fact that these particular joists, which were part of the bathroom floor, were holding up a cast-iron bathtub gave the discovery a special thrill.)

When structural members are bored through or hacked at or notched, the strength of an entire wall or ceiling can be compromised. You get slumping floors, sagging walls, in the worst of cases you may have a tub crush you while you do the dinner dishes, but always, you get cracks.

There are subtler ways remodelers can damage the stability of the house's structure. The weight of a new bathroom, for example, might place a lot of strain on a part of the house that's not used to it, and you'll see lots of cracking while the walls and ceiling below adjust to their new burden. Likewise, if a new window has been installed, without the addition of a load-bearing header above it, you'll see cracking aplenty as all the suddenly unsupported loads above the window press down.

Sometimes cracking happens when you change structural loads. For example, if you replace all your plaster walls with lighter-weight Sheetrock, you may get furious cracking as your floors, relieved of their heavy burden, slightly rise.

I finally traced my own cracking problem, in fact, to the recent removal of the wall between the living room and dining room. It wasn't a load-bearing wall, so I expected the effect on the house to be zilch, but an engineer pal of mine told me that in old houses, partition walls help stiffen the bearing walls they're attached to. With the partition gone, the bearing walls wobbled just enough to crack the plaster. He told me the house should adjust, and that no serious damage had been done.

The next time I saw Nick, I told him how the mystery of the cracks had been solved. He said he was happy, but that from now on, maybe I should come to see him a little less often.

"These once-a-week sessions are a bit too much," he said.

"But I think I'm making great strides," I said.

"No," said Nick. "I mean they're a bit too much for me."

Don't you love a shrink who can crack wise when the mood strikes him?

14
Vinnie Goes Macro

So last week the vivacious yet health-conscious Angela, love of my life, gets out of bed one day and decides it's time for the Agita household to go macrobiotic. No more ravioli stuffed with pesto gorgonzola, she says. No more gnocchi Bolognese. Forget the feather-light manicotti, and the *mostacciolli in ajo e ojo* sauce. Ixnay on the golden brown calzones. Eighty-six the fried polenta. Good-bye to the freaking *pasta e fagioli!!!* Instead, she says, we'll dine on a variety of boiled seaweeds and sautéed soybean curd.

My response was to recklessly stride toward the phone and order a deluxe, extra-cheese pepperoni pizza, right in front of her. I just didn't care. The pizza shop put me on hold, and while I was waiting, Angie made a suggestion.

"Make sure you order enough to share with your friends, the gnomes," she cooed, "because if you bring that pizza into this house, you're going to be living with them in the basement for the rest of the year."

When the pizza guy picked up, I asked him could he make a brown-rice-and-kelp stromboli, and acted all indignant when he said no way.

But I had to hand it to Angie, God bless her. She only wanted us to be healthy, to live a good long life together. So, I swallowed my pride, which was hard. Then I swallowed some kelp fritters, which was harder.

But hey, that's what love's all about. It helped, of course, that I was smuggling in contraband entrées from Luigi's Casa di Scungilli. I hid the stuff in a cooler in the basement, then slipped down after Ange had fallen asleep for a little late-night *mangia,* which, while certainly not biotic, was, no question about it, macro.

The other night, for example, I was lying in bed lusting after the double portion of linguini and mussels I'd stashed away. I waited for Angie's breathing to get slow and even, then I slipped out from under the covers and crept to the basement to retrieve my treat, then I bounded up the stairs to the kitchen, anticipating the rich forbidden pleasures in which I was about to indulge. But Angie cut me off at the microwave.

"I smell mussels," she said. "I smell cream sauce."

Thinking fast, I went stiff and bug-eyed, then I handed Ange the food. "Here's my homework, Mrs.

Lassiter," I said in a flat zombie drone, then I curled up on the dining room table and pretended to snore. Ange slammed the linguini down beside my head and told me to get my sleepwalking butt back down to the basement couch, then she headed back to bed.

"How did she hear me?" I wondered out loud. "She usually sleeps like a log."

"It's the squeaky floors, bonehead," she answered from the top of the stairs.

I winced in hapless chagrin. It's true. Our old oak floors have grown increasingly noisy over the last few years, groaning and squealing and creaking underfoot and generally driving Ange crazy. She'd been after me for months to do something about it, but I was never in the mood, and in the end the floors betrayed me. Don't let the same thing happen to you.

What hurts is, floor squeaks are easy to fix; the hard thing is that first you have to find them. And to do that, you need to know a little about the anatomy of your floor.

Let's start with the "joists." These beefy planks of framing lumber, which are visible overhead in an unfinished basement, are set, on edge, roughly sixteen or twenty-four inches apart, to form the structural framework, which supports the floor. The "subfloor"—made of plywood sheets in newer homes and solid boards in old ones—is nailed across the open joists to provide support for the "finish floor," which, when nailed to the subfloor, provides the surface you walk on.

A floor squeak results when one of these elements gets loose and sloppy and rubs against something it's not supposed to. (Which is not a good thing; just ask your nearest president of the U.S.A.)

First-floor squeaks are easy to find, especially if you have an unfinished basement, which should allow you to see the joists and the underside of the subfloor. Start by asking a helper to march around in the squeak zone while you watch from the basement below, training your flashlight along the top edge of the appropriate joist. If you spot gaps, or any signs of movement above the joist, that means the subfloor has lifted slightly from the floor framing. The fix for this is simple: Just brush some wood glue on either side of a tapered wood shim (which you can buy in bundles at a home center) and drive the shim between the joist and the subfloor until things snug up and the racket is silenced.

If the subfloor seems solidly attached to the joists, check out the joist's "bridging," which consists of short wood braces, nailed crosswise between the joists, to give the joists some side-to-side stability. Loose bridging can rub against the side of the joist, so look for popped nails in the ends of the crosspieces and drive them down solid.

No trouble visible from the basement? Then suspect that your squeak is caused by a finish floorboard that has separated slightly from the subfloor, and is rubbing against a nail or an adjacent board. From the first floor, locate the squeak by stepping on likely boards, then drill a small locater hole down through both the finish floor and the subfloor. Now go down to the basement and, using the locater hole as a guide, drive a wood screw up through the floor and into the finish board, drawing it tight against the subfloor. (Choose a screw that will penetrate no more than halfway into the finish board.) Finally, putty up the locater hole and the job's over.

Things get trickier, though, when you're dealing with squeaks in second-story floors (or in any floor, for that matter, that doesn't offer easy access from below). First, try a noninvasive approach. If the squeaks are caused by movement at the joints between floorboards, for example, try lubeing things up by sifting some talc or graphite powder into the cracks between the boards. Or, to relieve pressure between the floorboards, drive some glazier points—tiny metal triangles used to anchor windowpanes in their sashes—down between the boards, then pour in a little liquid floor wax.

No luck? Then you'll have to get butch with the squeaks, so gather up some thin, ring-shanked finish nails, your drill, and your hammer. If the loose floorboard is above a joist, just drill a pilot hole through the finish floor, using one of your ring-shanked nails as a bit, then nail the board tight to the joint. Of course, anyone who's ever studied the Chaos Theory of Handiness knows that the loose board never lies directly above the joist. So you'll probably have to drill angled pilot holes through adjacent squeaky boards and anchor them in the subfloor with your ring-shanked nails. In either case, countersink the nailheads, then fill the holes with matching putty.

A word of caution to those of an improvisational spirit: No matter how temptingly logical it seems, do not attempt to silence your floors with a spritz of WD-40. I tried this, and the results were unfortunate. Not that the silicone spray didn't immediately silence the squeaks—it did so nicely—but it also gave the floor an invisible, friction-free glazing, something I didn't consider until Angie's sweet old Aunt Lucretia, who was visiting for the weekend, started hydroplaning on her way to the john. She was already in motion when I spotted her through the bedroom doorway, doing a damn fine double axel and fighting like hell to nail her landing—Angie's people are all naturally athletic—but she lost her concentration, I guess, and took a fierce header into the laundry bin.

Which would have bought me swift banishment to the basement if I hadn't already been banished for my now notorious gnomicide. But I didn't intend to stay down there for long, because I know Ange. She is a sensual woman of deep gustatorial passions. Tofu cutlets could not hold her for long. So I hatched a plan to spring myself, at last, from the basement.

I have a small gas stove in the basement, see, and one night, after Angie finished her dinner of sprouts and seeds and went up to bed, I put on my apron and started to cook.

I boiled a pound of spinach-filled tortelloni in a big iron pot, then I heated extra-virgin olive oil in a heavy sauté pan, with minced garlic and a stick of butter. When the pasta was ready, I dumped it into a serving bowl and drenched it with the sauce, then I threw in a fistful of imported Parmesan cheese, which I'd grated by hand. A little ground sage, a dash of nutmeg, and, presto, olfactory bliss.

I carried the bowl over to the furnace and let the incredible aromas drift up into the intake vent. Then I turned on the blower fan and devilishly closed all the air ducts except the one leading to the room where Angie was trying to sleep. I figured five minutes would do the trick. I didn't want the pasta to cool.

Angie was wide awake and waiting when I arrived at the bedroom door with a steaming plate of *tortelloni al burro e formaggio* and a bottle of peppy zinfandel. She glared at me for a moment, then she dove into the pasta like a terrier going after a groundhog.

I joined her in the messy feasting, matching every slurp and smack of the lips. "Hey, Ange," I mumbled, with my mouth full, "you know what this reminds me of? That sexy feasting scene in *Tom Jones.*"

Ange looked up from her plate for a minute, and gazed thoughtfully at the ceiling. "Geeze, I don't know," she said, with exaggerated incredulity, "did Tom Jones sleep in a basement, with gnomes?"

❀ ❀ ❀

15
Regis the Mailman

It was another frigid morning in a freakishly cold and snowy November, one more leaden day in which no tools would be wielded. It had been months since Angie's "Gnomes Now!" edict had stripped me of my handy freedom and plunged me into the soul-sapping ennui that is the price one pays for suppressing one's natural how-to urges.

I was just beginning my second pot of java when I heard a commotion out on the front lawn. I stepped out on the porch and saw Regis, our mailman, standing at the end of the walk. He was waving some envelopes above his head.

"Here's your mail," he cried. "I'm not coming any closer!"

"What's wrong?" I shouted.

He gestured toward the sky. "It's too dangerous," he said. "This is as far as I go."

I rubbed my eyes and muttered to myself, wondering how I got such a chicken-hearted mailman. Rege won't cross a chemically treated lawn, for example. He trembles in the gaze of Mrs. Finelli's half-pint toothless shnauzer. And he lives in phobic dread of dying from a paper cut that gets infected. Postman's oath? Forget about it. If it sleets or hails, or if he senses the encroaching gloom of night, Rege stops his appointed rounds on the spot and runs straight home.

How he earned his mail-carrier's stripes, I'll never know. But I've been trying to help him work through his fears, and live up to the honorable tradition of his uniform. All he needs, I think, is a little push now and then, to show him that despite his jittery disposition, there's a can-do guy underneath. In any case, I wasn't about to let him give in to whatever nebulous terror had him paralyzed out there on the sidewalk. So I crossed my arms and demanded that he bring me my mail.

"But Mr. Agita," he cried, pointing skyward, "there's an incredibly dangerous—"

"Laugh at danger, Regis!" I shouted. "God's sakes man, you're a postal carrier!"

"But I could get killed!"

"Don't be ridiculous," I answered. "You're on my property. It's perfectly safe. What could happen to you here?"

"You don't understand," he said, pointing above my head, "there's a gigantic—"

"Yes, I do understand, Rege," I answered. "I understand that you can do it!"

Rege shook his head.

"Bring me that mail, Regey-boy!"

He didn't move.

"Come on, Regis. Nothing will hurt you."

"You promise?" he asked.

"Word of honor," said I. And finally, Rege stepped forward and made his way slowly down the walk. I was chanting "Regis-Regis" and he was smiling in triumph, but just as he was about to step up onto the porch there was a whooshing sound and a glittery flash and then an earth-shuddering thump, as a monstrous icicle—it was four feet long minimum and as thick as my thigh—dropped from the sky like a gigantic spearhead and planted itself six inches into the frozen turf at Rege's feet. Rege fainted dead away, and I couldn't blame him. One more step and that big nasty Popsicle would have skewered him like a rotisserie chicken.

I carried Rege inside, then went back out and looked at my house. All along the edge of the roof, a row of overgrown icicles hung like javelins, the longest ones stretching nearly ten feet, all of them thick-shafted, with needle-sharp tips.

Ange came out and stood beside me, horrified by the murderous icy curtain dangling from the eaves of our friendly little bungalow. "Where did they come from?" she gasped in horror. "What does it mean?"

I didn't want to say the words, but I couldn't hide the truth. "Honey," I said, "we have . . . an ice dam."

Ice dams, the homeowner's winter dread, begin when warm air inside the house rises to the attic and warms the underside of the roof, causing the snow above to melt. The melted snow runs down the roof until it hits the colder overhanging eaves, which have no warm room air below them, and here the snowmelt freezes solid.

In time, the refrozen snow jams the gutters and begins to mass in a hump or "dam" all along the eaves, which blocks any runoff of melted snow. Some of that runoff dribbles over the dam as it freezes and forms, inch by inch, the stalactitelike icicles of the sort that almost bisected Rege.

But most of the melting snow pools on the roof behind the dam, where it can seep under your shingles and into your house. Even in mild cases, this infiltrating moisture can damage wooden rafters and roof decking. In worse cases, it can send a waterfall cascading down your interior walls, damaging plaster and possessions and electrical wiring.

There are a number of ways to prevent the cruel heartbreak of ice damming. You can string low-voltage electrical cables along the eaves to warm that crucial section of the roof and prevent runoff from refreezing. And if you ever reroof your house, you can tell your contractor to install a special waterproof barrier beneath the shingles along the eaves. Once this rubbery stuff is rolled on, it provides a watertight membrane so dependable that even if an ice dam forms, and water pools on top of it, your house should stay snug and dry.

But the best way to prevent an ice dam is to give your attic a thick blanket of insulation. That'll keep your warm inside air from heating the roof, so the whole thaw-and-refreeze cycle never gets started.

Fine. But what if, say, you choose to take the money you'd saved for attic insulation and spent it on that impromptu junket to Atlantic City. (So you lost all your cash and your attic went without and now you're plagued with dammed-up ice. Who can ever take from you the memory of Norm Crosby's kooky comic stylings, or the magic of Ferrante and Teicher playing "Stairway to Heaven"?)

Well, here's what I did. First, I climbed up into the attic and spread plastic sheeting under the eaves, hoping to catch any drips before they could do damage to the house below. Then, to relieve my gutters from the strain of all that overhanging ice, and reduce the dangers to people below, I went outside and used a long clothes prop to knock down as many icicles as I could. If you try this yourself, be very careful. The ice will ricochet and explode upon impact into shrapnellike fragments that can damage anything in its path—a porch roof, a parked car, a picture window, or the next-door-neighbors' innocent and trusting basset hound. (You won't believe what vet bills are like anymore, and let me tell you, you don't want to have to face some sad-eyed bowser, staring at you with hurtful confusion from inside one of those big plastic cones.)

Another thing to remember: A chunk of solid ice falling twenty or thirty feet can put your lights out for good. So wear a hard hat and good eye protection. Or better yet, call in a crew of professional roofers. They'll safely remove the overhanging ice, then chip channels through the ice dam itself, allowing the melting snow to drain easily off the roof.

By the time I'd finished tending to my ice problems, Rege had come around. He was wrapped in a blanket, and Angie was feeding him soup, but when I asked him how he felt, he snapped, "I'm never coming back here again."

"You have to, Regis," I answered. "You're the mailman."

"No, if I keep coming back I'll die here."

"Don't get carried away," I said.

"He has a point," said Angie.

"You're talking about the ditch incident," I said groaning. "That was a freak accident." What happened was, I had to dig a six-foot trench in the front yard to run a new water line, and I tarped it off at night in case it rained. Unfortunately, I used an old camouflage tent as the tarp, not taking into account Regis's Coke-bottle glasses. Anyway, he fell in, and accidentally maced himself and got his mail all muddy and I heard about that for months.

"What about the time you almost fried him on the front porch?" snapped Angie. "You can still see the outline of his rubber-soled shoes on the steps. And what kind of idiot hot-wires the mailbox, anyway?"

I had her there. "I admit there are a few bugs to be worked out," I said, "but think of it Angie, a few small adjustments, and all winter long, heated mail."

When Rege heard that he began to whimper, so I knew some decisive action was in order.

I grabbed him by the collar, shoved him to the doorway, and pushed him through the door.

"You're a mailman, Rege," I cried. "Be true to your calling! Deliver the mail!"

Angie just sat there with her arms folded. "Weren't you a little tough on him?" she growled.

"It was just what the kid needed," I replied. "A little push. A little tough love. I know what I'm doing here, Ange. After all, you know I'm an excellent judge of character."

Ange's delicate nostrils flared.

"Angie, Angie, Angie," I said with a chuckle. "He's a postal worker. They don't come any more stable than that. They have to pass a test to get that job, for crimeny's sake. So just trust me here, okay? Someday, when we least expect it, that young man will come back and express, in no uncertain terms, his complete appreciation for what I've done."

Like I said, I'm an excellent judge of character.

16
Vinnie "The Tool" Agita

W here would you like to start today?" asked my shrink, Nick, eager to plumb once more the wounded, yearning handyman inside me.

"I need some help with a life decision," I said. "It could be a turning point for me."

"I'll do my best," he said. "How can I help?"

"It's about identity," I said.

"That's a very basic issue," Nick replied.

"Yeah, the whole 'who am I, where am I going' thing. . . ."

"Exactly."

"It's been on my mind a lot."

"Then let's explore it."

I nodded and gathered my thoughts. "I feel a strong need to know who I am," I said, "to know what I believe in and what really matters to me."

"Those are key questions," said Nick, his hands folded and his knuckles pressed against his lips.

"I want the world to know the real me."

"But first," said Nick, with a knowing grin, "you have to *find* the real you."

"Bingo!" I replied. "And that's where I need your help."

Nick smiled. "That's really what therapy is all about," he said, "but I have to warn you, it doesn't happen overnight. Like any human being, you are infinitely complex, layered with insights, contradictions, rich emotional textures, and damaging self-delusions. Those things must be sorted out and clarified and contemplated. It takes time. It takes courage. It takes unflinching honesty. But most of all, it takes a real desire to change."

I drummed my fingers thoughtfully on the padded leather arms of the swivel chair. "Really?" I said. "I was thinking a really good nickname would do it."

Dr. Nick cocked his head and squinted. "A nickname?" he repeated.

"Yeah," I said. "What better way to define yourself? Look at Jesse 'The Body' Ventura. Guy has nothing going but a perfect nickname, and he rides it all the way to the governor's mansion. Name recognition, that's what it's all about."

"And you think a good nickname will bring you similar success?" Nick inquired.

"It's not about success," I said. "It's all about being me."

"So it's part of your attempt to define yourself."

"Yeah. And to promote the handy values I cherish."

"Handy values?"

I nodded. "My handy credo," I said.

"You have a credo for your hobby?"

I balled my hand into a fist and bit down hard until the knuckles went white. It was a while before I could bring myself to speak, and then it was in a hoarse, faltering whisper.

"If you hear nothing else, hear this," I croaked. "Handiness is not a *hobby*. It's not a *pastime* or *recreation*. It's a worldview. It's a gestalt. Handiness is a beacon, a guiding vision; it's the crowbar with which we pry the manhole cover from life's inscrutable mysteries, and the halogen floodlight that brightens the long dark night of the soul."

The sudden burst of passion seemed to startle Nick a little. "I meant no offense," he said. "It's just that those how-to shows on TV seem to be geared to people who enjoy do-it-yourself stuff as, you know, a hobby."

"Oh please," I cried, "do not mix me up with those TV how-to hucksters. They're selling us a lie, Doc, one big candy-coated handy fantasy."

"They seem very good at what they do—"

"Oh yeah, flawless," I jibed. "Look! Norm Abrams,

that hefty flannel-clad megahandyman, just built a full-scale plywood replica of Chartres Cathedral using only his turbo-powered biscuit joiner and his laser-guided radial arm saw (the one with infrared night-vision systems and full stealth technology).

"Somebody, please, gag me with a ball peen hammer. This is fantasy, Nick. I mean, ask yourself: Did you ever see one of these guys bend a nail, or staple his sleeve to a stud, or get his head stuck between stairway balusters, or wall up Mrs. Finelli's wandering geriatric poodle and have to rip down a weekend's worth of dry-walling to set him free?"

Nick's eyebrows arched. "Am I hearing some professional rivalry?" he asked.

"It's not about jealousy, Doc," I answered. "It's about truth. It's about who gets to define the real nature of handiness. Those TV guys want to keep it all sanitized and corporate and dorky."

Nick smirked slightly.

"Admit it, you think handiness is dorky," I said. "But handiness isn't dorky. It's decisive and creative and, in the right situation, subversive. What better way to poke your finger in the eye of the bloodless virtual society rising all around us? Nothing virtual about swinging a sledge, Doc, or tackling a toilet clog, or getting that fleshy little web of skin between the thumb and forefinger caught in the gears of a C-clamp."

"So, if I'm hearing you clearly," Nick replied, "you're saying it's more than a diversion."

"It's primal, Doc," I answered. "It's a defining human trait. The anthropologists will tell you—tool savvy is what sets us apart from the monkeys. Here it is in a nutshell: We are never more human than when we fix, when we struggle to rebuild and reshape the world around us. That's my credo. These are the values I would like to project. So please, since it's my ninety bucks paying for this hour, can we just discuss the freaking nickname thing?"

"I think there's no way around it," Nick replied.

I nodded in satisfaction and pulled out my list.

"I have some ideas written down," I said. "Why don't I read them off, and you give me your reaction."

"Go ahead," Nick said.

"Don't pull any punches."

"Fire away."

"Some of these are rough. . . ."

"Just read, Vinnie," he said.

I nodded and smoothed the list on my lap. "Here goes," I said. "First one's pretty straightforward: Vinnie 'The Tool' Agita."

Nick's brow wrinkled in disdain. "Sounds like a seventies porno star," he said.

"That was just a warm-up," I replied. "How about The Gangster of Handy Love?"

Nick frowned. "What else do you have?"

"The Raging Bull of Home Repair?"

Nick stroked his chin.

"The Hunka-Hunka-Handy Love? Baron Von Fixmeister? The Godfather of Do-It-Yourself Soul?"

Nick smiled weakly and tapped his pen on his lips. "Let me think it over," he said, "and in the meanwhile, why don't we talk about how things are going between you and Angela. Is she still making you sleep in the basement?"

"Affirmative," I said, "and banning me from all handy exploits whatsoever. . . ."

"So, I'm assuming you haven't been intimate with your wife since the incident with the gnomes?"

Talk about your neb-noses. "No offense, Doc," I said, with a chastising frown, "but is that an appropriate question? I mean, come on: Hey, Vinnie, gettin' any?"

"Vincent," Nick said, scowling, "this is therapy."

"But crimeny," I said, "I didn't know it would get so personal."

Nick shrugged. "You don't have to answer if you don't want to," he said.

I mulled it over. Sure it was embarrassing, but at the outset, I'd promised Ange I'd be unflinchingly honest, so I really had no choice.

"Okay," I said, "I'll tell the truth. Ange hasn't let me near her in weeks. I've been banned from frolicking in the boudoir, I've been banned from cavorting with my tools. I've got no noisy, sweaty fun happening in my life whatsoever."

"You must feel a tremendous sense of frustration," suggested Nick.

"It's building up inside me, Doc," I carped. "I'm trying to tow the line, but I feel like I'm going to explode."

"It doesn't surprise me," Nick said. "But you won't ever solve your problems by hiding behind some false handy persona. You're not the Gangster of Handy Love, or the Dalai Lama of Do-It-Yourself, or The Drill Sergeant, or any of those things. Pretending that you are is only an attempt to dodge the genuine and complex feelings of the real Vinnie, who's hiding deep inside. That's the goal of our work here together—to find that wounded inner Vinnie, and see what he's afraid of."

Nick went on like that for a good three or four minutes, making references to my hopes, my fears, my dreams, my pain, yada yada, and otherwise generally hogging the floor. I politely pretended to listen, but my attention had subtly shifted to the light brown water mark billowing like a beige carnation above our heads.

"I know you don't like me to mention this," I said, when Nick had finally finished, "but that stain has been bothering me since the first time I came here. I really wish you'd let me climb up there and give it a look-see."

Nick dropped his notebook to his lap. "This is my point exactly," he said. "Every time we get close to striking a resonant chord, you sabotage the conversation and veer off into the refuge of handy talk."

"But you could have a real problem brewing up there," I replied. "Water leaks can do serious damage. They can rot out the framing, they can attract wood-munching bugs, they can soak your insulation and even cause rust and dangerous shorts in your electrical system."

"I'm not letting you go anywhere near that stain," Nick insisted. "It would defeat the purpose of all our work."

"I hear what you're saying," I said, "and I wouldn't push it except I know there's a bathroom up above us, right?"

"Yes, there is," Nick replied.

"House this old," I said, "I bet you still have the original cast-iron tub."

"As a matter of fact, I do," Nick admitted.

"I saw one of those fall on a guy once. Flattened him like a Pringle."

"The tub is not going to fall."

"Your mouth to God's ears," I said, "but if that leaking water has rotted out the floor joists . . ."

Nick glanced at his watch. "We have to stop now," he said. "Same time next week?"

"Sounds good," I replied, "but before I leave, could you get me a copy of the last bill? I seem to have mislaid it."

"My files are in the storage room," said Nick. "It'll take me a minute to dig it out."

The moment Nick left the room I snatched a Hi-Lighter pen from his desk and stood on the seat of his chair. Stretching as far as I could, I was just able to reach the ceiling, and outline the edge of the stain in faint yellow ink.

When he came back I was waiting in the doorway. "Here's the bill," he said. "Hope I got your name right. I never even asked—is it *Vinnie* with an *i-e* on the end or just a *y?*"

I thought it over, then grabbed a pen from Nick's desk and scribbled a quick doodle.

"What's this?" Nick asked. "It looks like a wrench and a plunger crossed like swords on a shield."

"That's not a shield," I explained. "It's the lid of a toilet seat. From now on, just draw that little picture when you make out my bill."

"I don't follow."

"I'm taking your advice," I said. "I'm dropping the nickname idea, and instead, I'm going with a symbol. It's more poetic; it's pure."

"But what do I call you?" asked Nick.

"It's just a trial thing," I said, "but for the time being, let's go with The Handyman Formerly Known as Vinnie."

17
Aliens

Last night I was in the garage, cleaning some paintbrushes with turpentine, when, out of nowhere, I had one of those recovered memories. You know how it goes—you suffer a traumatic experience, you bury it in your subconscious, then one day, after working for hours with volatile solvents in cramped, unventilated quarters, it all comes raging to the surface. Happens all the time on TV.

Anyway, it was suddenly very clear to me that sometime in the past year, I'd been abducted by invaders from another galaxy: gray little bulb-headed guys with stick-figure bodies, lipless beaks, and fleshy suction cups on the tips of their long spindly fingers. Don't get me wrong, I'm not the kind of guy who judges by appearances, but

I'm trying to paint a picture: Chippendale dancers, these guys ain't.

I don't know what drew them to me. They simply showed up in the bedroom one night, did some wiggly moon-man mumbo jumbo—which instantly put me in a groggy stupor—then hoisted me up to the mother ship on a beam of golden light.

When my head finally cleared, I found myself inside their saucer, strapped to a cold metal examination table, with three bug-eyed space weasels leaning over me, eyeing me like I was a bullfrog in a high school biology lab. "Lemme guess," I chuckled, just to break the tension. "You guys wouldn't be here to represent the Lollipop Guild, would you?"

The space guys didn't crack a smile. Instead, one of them, stepped forward and telepathically introduced himself. His name was Harriet Tubman. (I think they had hastily studied our history and assumed the names of highly admired figures, hoping this would pacify their earthling captives and make us more malleable subjects.)

Anyway, Harriet was holding a razor-tipped stainless steel probe the size of a shish kebab skewer.

"Relax," he said as he tickled my nostrils with the probe, "I just want to reach up inside your sinus cavities and snip off a little chunk of your cerebellum. You might feel a pinch."

But just as Harriet powered up the laser-powered brain-snipper, there was a soft pop, then the lights went out.

"Damn," said Harriet, "blew another fuse."

"Does that happen often?" I inquired.

"Too often," Harriet replied as crew members scrambled to get the lights back on. When the room was lit again, Harriet pressed me back down on the table.

"Sorry about that," he said. "Now, try not to sneeze. . . ."

"Anything for science," I said as Harriet began to slip the probe up my snout, "but before you go any further, you really ought to do something about that electrical problem."

Harriet and his homely chums exchanged puzzled glances.

"Well, look around," I said, pointing to a snarl of power lines and cables snaking all over the room. "You've got extension cords stretched everywhere, all your outlets are overloaded with cheap, multiplug adapters. I mean, one little power surge, a spark or two, and fooom! This saucer goes up like an Unidentified Flying Ford Pinto."

"You really think it's that dangerous?" asked Harriet's sidekick, Alex Trebek.

"It indicates an inadequacy in your electrical system," I replied. "It's a basic handy no-no."

"It does look a bit suspect," said Harriet, "but crimeny, we have so many gadgets—the ray guns, the teleporter beams, the antigravity generators, the Presto Fry Baby. . . ."

"It's a space catastrophe waiting to happen," I said. "But if you let me up from this table, I can straighten it out for you in no time."

Harriet turned to the third space geek, who was leaning against a control panel. "What's your opinion?" he asked.

"We have been blowing a lot of fuses lately," Santa Claus replied. Harriet thought it over.

"How long will it take?" he asked.

"Depends on the problem," I said. "I can't tell you until I get a look at the power box."

"Okay," he said, "here's the deal. We let you up just long enough to examine the box. But no funny stuff. And when you're finished, it's back on the table and the needle goes right up the schnozola."

I flashed him a big smile. "Ten-four, Harriet," I replied, "my gray matter is your gray matter. But I could use a little help, so which of you bug-eyed bad boys is handy?"

"I'd be glad to help," said Harriet, "as long as you don't expect too much. Afraid I'm all thumbs." (A quick glance at Harriet's knuckly paws showed him to be a literalist.)

"That's the spirit, Tubster," I replied. "Now, show me to the service panel." Harriet nodded and called up to the bridge, "Hey, Jehova, open the doors to the mechanical room!"

Seconds later two metal doors slid open, and Harriet led me down into the bowels of the ship and back to the cluttered mechanical room. I found the power box mounted on a wall in the corner, between the hyperspace engines and stacks of old alien girlie mags.

"Okay, Harriet," I said, "I'm going to give you a quick and very useful overview of how your electrical system works. It all starts here, in the power box, or service panel. See that thick cable snaking down the wall? That encloses the 'service conductors,' which deliver power from the utility company—or, in your case, from that big throbbing chunk of plutonium over there. Electricity flows into this box through that cable, and the box distributes it to the different circuits, which supply your saucer with power."

I could almost hear Harriet's beach ball–size brain whirring as he digested the information, and he gasped in wonder as I flipped open the service panel's metal door to expose the neat rows of black plastic switches nestled inside.

"Circuit breakers," I said. "Each circuit has one. When these switches sense that too much current is being drawn through a circuit—and that a dangerous situation is arising—they automatically trip and instantly stop the flow of electricity through that circuit."

"It computes," muttered Harriet.

"Some systems have screw-in fuses instead of circuit breakers," I told him. "Fuses have a small metal conductor inside that simply melts when too much current is drawn. That interrupts the circuit and immediately stops the flow of power."

"Same principle as the circuit breaker," said Harriet.

"Exactly," I agreed, "but breakers can be reset, while fuses must be replaced."

"Mysterious," muttered H, "yet self-evident . . ."

"Here's the thing to remember," I said. "Notice that each circuit breaker is stamped with letters and numerals: This one says 15A; that one says 20A. *A* stands for amperes, and the numerals tell us how many amps the circuit protected by that breaker can safely carry. Exceed 15 amps on a 15-amp breaker, for example, and kablooie, the breaker slams on the breaks."

"As if it had a mind of its own . . . ," Harriet mused.

"Another thing. Notice how most of the breakers in the box occupy only one horizontal slot? Those breakers are all attached to 120-volt runs. Most of the house is serviced by 120-volt circuits."

"What about those double-size breakers, which take up two slots?" Harriet inquired.

"Those big boys are guarding beefy 240-volt circuits," I answered, "each of which powers a single, heavy-duty appliance: a water heater, an electric stove, a clothes dryer, or your furnace. If you have fuses, 240-volt circuits are guarded by double cartridges snapped into a removable block."

"I find this sense of order very elegant," said Harriet. "It all makes such beautiful sense."

"I know," I said, "it's the wonder of handiness. But let's stay focused. There are two reasons a breaker repeatedly trips. The first, and most serious, is the presence of a short circuit."

"That sounds dangerous," he grumbled.

"It could start a fire," I replied. "Here's how to find one. After your breaker trips, unplug any heavy-drain appliances—steam irons, space heaters, hair dryers, electric frying pans—then go to the panel and reset the breaker. If it doesn't trip right away, the short might be in one of the appliances.

Next, plug in each appliance, one at a time. If the breaker trips when you turn on, say, that power hog of a karioke machine I saw up in the control room, you've probably found the culprit."

"We only use the karioke for cultural research," said Harriet.

"Yeah," I said, "I guess you guys aren't much for sing-alongs, being lipless and all. But anyway, if the circuit breaker continues to trip with nothing plugged into any outlets, you probably have a problem with the wiring itself—frayed insulation, for example, or a loose wire inside a metal connection box. Either way, shorts are nothing to fool with, and if I thought that was your problem, I'd send you right up to the teleporter room and tell you to beam in a pro, pronto."

"But you don't think it's a short?"

"I think you have a simpler and more common problem: an overloaded circuit, and that's what we need to check."

"How can I be of service?" Harriet inquired.

"You can send a mind-gram up to Alex Trebek, and tell him to plug a lamp into that problem outlet," I said. Harriet's forehead rumpled as he transmitted, then he smiled.

"Light's on," he said.

I nodded and started flipping each 120-volt breaker to the off position. When I tripped breaker five, Harriet interrupted me. "Alex says the light just went out."

"Good," I replied. "That means circuit five is our baby. Look here, it's a 15-amper. It's 120 volts. Remember that, okay?" I left circuit five in the off position but reset all the other breakers. "Okay, done," I said. "Now let's go upstairs."

Back in the control room, I asked Harriet and his crew to unplug everything from all the outlets. Meanwhile, I drew a rough diagram of the room, upon which I marked the locations of every switch, outlet, and electrical fixture in the room. Then I borrowed a small desk lamp made from a globe of Saturn and systematically plugged it into every single outlet in the place.

"What are you doing?" asked Harriet.

"I'm mapping the circuit," I said. "We know no power is flowing through circuit five, so any outlet that doesn't light the lamp is part of that circuit."

As I worked, Harriet marked my findings on the diagram. After mapping all the outlets, we did the same for the switches by flipping them on and documenting the ones that did not work.

When we finished with the control room, we mapped out the bridge, the galley, the heads, the game room. And when we had all of circuit five diagrammed, we performed the same procedure with every circuit on the ship.

"This is tedious work," griped Harriet.

"Sometimes handiness can be a grind," I said, "but diagramming your circuits is something every starship captain or earthling homeowner should do. (And don't forget to map out porches, garages, basements, lunar modules, etc.) Sure, it can kill a Saturday, but when you're finished, you have a detailed portrait of your entire circuit structure, and that can help you get the most out of your electrical system."

"How so?" asked Harriet.

"If you'll go down and turn on all the circuits," I said as I snatched the circuit map from his hand, "the answer will soon be clear."

As Harriet went down to the service panel, I worked my way around the ship, plugging in all the appliances exactly as they had been before. When Harriet came back, I explained what I was up to.

"According to the diagram, circuit five feeds juice to all the outlets in these two walls, to the eerie luminous floor panels, and to that wall switch, which powers the disco ball. Now all we need to do is calculate the total number of amps being drawn by all the stuff feeding off that circuit. If it adds up to more than 15 amps, we know we have an overload."

"That sounds complicated," said Harriet.

"It's a snap," I replied. "Most appliances clearly list their amp rating, either on a nameplate or a stamped label. See here: The death ray draws 3 amps, the asteroid shield draws 4, the vibrating Barcalounger gobbles up 1.5. . . ."

"But look at my Crock-Pot," said Harriet. "It says '360 watts.'"

"Don't let that throw you. You can easily convert watts to amps using this simple formula."

Then I pulled a pencil from my pocket and scribbled the formula on the spaceship wall:

$$\text{Watts} \div \text{Volts} = \text{Amps}$$

"Remember, this is a 120-volt circuit," I reminded him, "so, 360 watts divided by 120 volts equals 3 amps."

"Science," whispered Harriet. "How I love science."

It took us only a moment to crunch the numbers: the result—a constant load of 14 amps on circuit number five. "That's pushing it on a 15-amp circuit," I said.

"What can we do?"

"You could add a new circuit," I told him. "But there might be a simpler and cheaper fix. This is where the circuit map really comes in handy."

I spread the map out on a console. "Our problem is, circuit five is pushed to the limit. But lookee over here. Circuit three has some room: only 12 amps being drawn through a 20-amp line. And circuit seven has a few amps to spare. Ditto circuits two and twelve."

With all the circuits mapped so clearly, it was a cinch to rearrange all the appliances so that electrical loads were spread out over all the circuits.

"Voila!" I exclaimed. "No more overload. Your circuits are now nicely balanced, and circuit five has plenty of room to spare. So you shouldn't be tripping any more breakers, as long as you don't plug in anything ridiculous."

As I was speaking, the lights went out.

"What happened?" cried a voice from the bridge. It was Abraham Lincoln. "I just plugged in my sunlamp and kaflooey!"

I turned to Harriet in the darkness. "Don't take this the wrong way," I said, "but do you guys actually tan?"

As I'd hoped, Harriet was so pleased with my handy intercession that he agreed to keep his surgical needles way clear of my beezer. Instead, he took me up to the bridge and let me steer the saucer for a while. So I throttled up and put that space buggy through its paces. First I did a few speed-of-light laps around the equator, then I circled the North Pole, zigzagged through the Pyramids, buzzed the Eiffel Tower, and finally made a hairpin U-bie and zipped back east across the Atlantic.

"Slow down," said Harriet as I veered left at the Carolina coast and cruised south toward Florida. "You want to stay to your right here. Stay right, Vinnie. Vinnie, right! My God, go right, go right . . . !!!"

When I came to, I was on the living room sofa. Ange was dabbing my forehead with a cool damp cloth.

"I found you in the garage," she muttered. "You were yammering deliriously."

"What day is it?" I asked. "How long have I been away?"

"Forget what day it is," she snapped. "Who the hell is Harriet?"

18
The Inkblot

walked into Nick's office a couple of weeks later.
Nick was sitting in his swivel chair with a stack of
eight-by-ten flash cards on his lap.

"I'd like to try an exercise today," he said. "You've
heard of the Rorschach test?"

"Yeah," I answered, "the inkblot thing."

"That's right," said Nick. "Remember, there are no
wrong answers—whatever you say will help us get a
sense of what's going on inside you. The important
thing is to answer immediately."

"Got it."

"Okay," he said, "let's try card one. What do you
see?" he asked.

It was a dark blue blob. I stared and stared. I saw a

dark blue blob. After thirty seconds of silence, Nick tossed the card on the floor.

"Let's try another one," he said, "and remember, quick impressions . . ."

He held up the card. "Remind you of anything?" he asked.

I nodded. "Reminds me a little of card one," I said.

Nick scratched his forehead impatiently. "Vinnie," he said, "we aren't going to get anywhere here if you don't at least try."

"I'm sorry," I said. "I'll try harder."

Nick nodded and held up the third card.

"Sistine Chapel!" I shouted.

Nick frowned.

"The Comet Kahoutek!" I cried.

"Vinnie . . ."

"Man's Inhumanity to Man!"

Nick tossed the cards to the floor and gave me a sulky stare.

"Sorry, Doc," I said, "but you know what those inkblots really remind me of? That big brown water blotch on the ceiling above your head. It worries me more each time I see it. Please let me check it out for you."

"Vinnie," said Nick, "this total inability to ignore even the slightest chance to be handy is why you're here. Forget the blotch. It's probably been there for years."

I rose from my chair and crossed the room. "Can I show you something?" I said. "Stand here beside me."

Nick stood up and I pointed at the stain, which was now directly above us. "See that faint yellow line? I drew that line last week."

"You drew on my ceiling?"

"You're not looking, Doc," I said. "When I drew that line, I traced the exact outline of the perimeter of the stain. You can see that the brown stain has spread beyond the line. That means the leak that's causing that stain is active. At the very least, you have a big patch of heavy, soggy plaster right above your chair. And believe me, you don't want that load crashing down on your head just as you're trying to convince some poor depressed paranoid type that the sky isn't falling."

"That does sound dangerous," Nick allowed.

I sensed a little give. "Just let me make sure the plaster is stable," I said. "If it is, I'll never mention the blotch again."

"You promise?"

"Handyman's Honor," I replied.

"All right," Nick huffed. "Let's get past this. I'll go get a stepladder."

Once upon the ladder, I could see a definite bulge in the plaster. I poked the bulge gently with my finger. Then I punched it lightly with my fist.

The punch was all it took. In a flash, the plaster let loose from the lath boards and crashed, with a leaden thud, to the carpeted floor below. Next came a black slurry of standing water, plaster dust, and soot. Nick danced back smartly but not smartly enough to keep the slop from staining his Hush Puppies, and when I toppled off the ladder it was Doctor Nick who broke my fall.

"Get off!" he cried. "Our time is up!"

"That whole ceiling's weak," I said as I helped him to his feet. "Like it or not, you've got a handy decision to make."

"I'm not going to let you work on my ceiling," he said. "That would only be feeding your addiction."

"That's one way of looking at it," I said. "But let's examine things with a clinical eye: You've seen for yourself, I have handy urges that are being dangerously stifled. I'm probably heading for a breaking point. And what better way to safely vent some handy steam than in a controlled setting, under the watchful supervision of a professional, such as you?"

Nick gave me a wary scowl.

"Think of it as a new kind of treatment," I continued. "I wrestle with my demons right here in front of you. . . ."

Nick's gaze drifted off to the distance. "That's actually an interesting thought," he replied.

"You observe it all firsthand," I said.

"We might even stumble on some new therapeutic insights," he mumbled to himself.

"Maybe you'll write a paper."

"We might be helping others. . . ."

"That's the spirit, Doc," I said, leaping to my feet. "Why don't I get started?"

"Hold on," said Nick. "I don't think Angela would like this."

I dismissed Nick's concern with a wave and a chuckle. "Angela wants a husband she can live with," I said. "And if working off my handy ya-ya's makes me a better man, then where's the harm? Besides, technically, you aren't allowed to squeal to Angie, right? Doctor-patient confidentiality and all, right?"

Nick rubbed his chin as he gazed at the ceiling. The hook was set, I could tell.

"How big a job is it?" he asked.

"Hard to say," I answered. "You never know where the chain of handiness might lead. Best case, we find the leak quickly, fix it, then patch up the hole."

"You can fix the ceiling that quickly?"

"Depends on the state of the plaster," I explained. "It's definitely sagging. But the surface looks intact. We might be able to save it."

I explained to Nick that in old houses like his, plaster walls hang on a framework of thin wooden slats called lath. The lath was nailed across the studs, and when the fresh plaster was spread over the lath, it oozed between the narrow spaces between the slats. Once these oozing blobs hardened, they gripped the lath like chubby little fingers. The pros call these blobs the "keys." The keys hold the plaster fast to the lath. But over time, due to vibrations or age or, as in Nick's case, the infiltration of moisture, the keys weaken and crumble. When that happens, plaster sags from ceilings and bulges from walls.

"Can you fix it?" Nick asked.

I shrugged. "Most guys will tell you to tear it down

and start fresh with new drywall," I said. "But some-times, if the plaster hasn't crumbled too badly, you can simply reattach it to the lath with special screws."

I told Nick about the screws. They have very sharp points, thin shafts, and a soft plastic collar around the head. The fix is simple. You drive the screws through the loose plaster and into the lath with a power drill fit-ted with a screwdriver bit. Go slowly—if you drive the screw too deeply you'll crack the plaster. The goal is to snug the plaster up to the lath, letting the soft plastic collar cushion the pressure. Use lots of screws. Once the plaster feels solid again, cover all the screw heads with Spackle, then sand and paint, and you've saved yourself the misery of plaster demolition.

"I like the idea of saving the plaster," said Nick.

"I'll do everything I can to make it new again," I said.

"How long do you think it will take?"

"If we're lucky," I estimated, "one day, tops."

Nick nodded. "Okay, it's a deal," he said. "But we have to have some guidelines."

And then Nick started yammering again about lim-its and accountability and trust and so on, but I had other things on my mind, such as, where to lay my hands on some tools.

19
Alphonse

was up on a ladder at Dr. Nick's, pulling Romex cable through holes I'd drilled in the wall studs, and fearlessly baring my soul.

"We used to be soul mates," I explained to Nick, who was sitting near the base of the ladder, on a five-gallon bucket of drywall mud. "We used to frolic together, we used to gaze for hours into each other's eyes. We couldn't keep our paws off each other. Now, it's almost like we're strangers."

Nick took a deep breath, adjusted his hard hat, then soberly replied, "It's a difficult thing when conflict shatters the intimacy between a husband and a wife."

"What wife?" I replied. "I'm talking about my relationship with Alphonse, my cat."

Nick dropped his notebook on his lap. "I don't do cats, Vinnie," he said.

"But you have to help me," I pleaded. "It's draining the joy from my life."

"Look at that!" he cried, tapping his watch with his pen. "Our time's all up. But speaking of draining people, can we please talk about this project? All this mess is disruptive."

For a moment, Nick and I fell quiet as we surveyed the handy-landscape before us. In the three short weeks I'd labored here, Nick's office had been transformed into a field of glorious handy battle. All the plaster that had once made up the walls and ceilings had been reduced to rolling hummocks of dusty rubble. The gutted walls now revealed all the house's hidden mysteries—the dangling electrical wires, the raw structural framing, the diagonal sheathing boards that formed the home's exterior shell, the old copper water pipes zigzagging between the framing, and the rickety steel ductwork rising between the studs.

"Awesome, isn't it, Doc," I whispered, "peering into the Heart of Handy Darkness?"

"What do you mean?" asked Nick.

"We've ripped away the illusion of safe, civilized walls, and now we're face-to-face with something primal."

"Vinnie," said Nick, "it's just a wall. And I don't understand why you had to tear down all this plaster just to fix a water spot in the ceiling."

"Think in terms of therapy," I suggested. "You ask probing questions. The answers lead to more questions, the questions lead you deeper and deeper toward some irreducible truth. It's a difficult and disruptive journey. Things get worse before they get better. But in the end—clarity! Insight! Something gets fixed! That's my handy philosophy in a nutshell! So you and I aren't all that different. We both try to cast a little light into the shadows, and when we find problems we try to set them right."

"I'm having trouble applying all this to the wall. . . ."

"Okay, I'll speak plainly. First I tore down the ceiling plaster—it was too far gone to be saved. Then I started searching for the source of the water that caused the famous stain. I found it—a supply pipe to the upstairs bathroom had a pinhole leak. It trickled along some pipes and floor joists to a low point under the tub, then dripped down onto the plaster."

"And you fixed that, right?"

"Right."

"Then why didn't you just repair the ceiling and quit?"

"Because, with the ceiling plaster down, I saw signs of other water damage. Wood rot had weakened the corner post in that end of the wall, and seeping water had rusted out the electrical connections inside a junction box right down below. I tried to fix that first, but when I opened up the box I didn't like the look of things at all. We're talking about some ancient wiring here—

probably original to the house—and in those days they used wires clad only in woven fabric insulation. Over time, that insulation grows brittle and crumbles. For all I knew, the whole wall was smoking like a grill at Sizzlers. I had no choice but to be certain. So I gutted all the plaster and ripped out all the old wiring, which I'm now replacing with this safe, modern Romex."

"I guess that's smart," Nick consented. "But I think I want to be here from now on when you're working."

"But you get so anxious," I said.

"I'll handle it," he said. "I just want this house put back together."

When I got home, Alphonse was on the sofa, pretending to be asleep, but the irritated twitch in his nostrils gave him away.

I got right to the point: "We need to talk, Alphonse," I said. "I feel as though I'm putting more into our relationship than I'm getting out."

Alphonse grumbled softly, keeping his eyes tightly shut.

"Damn it, Alphonse," I said, "if you want this relationship to work you've got to fight for it!"

Alphonse let out a weary sigh and opened his eyes. Then, with an exaggerated effort, he hopped off the couch and disappeared behind it.

I slept fitfully that night and woke all mopey and depressed. I mean, if a man can't count on his pet, what can he count on?

"He's so distant, so cold," I told Angie the next morning. "I'm a giver, Ange, but all he does is take, take, take."

"Maybe your relationship is in transition," she answered, without lifting her eyes from the newspaper, "or maybe he's grown and you haven't; or maybe you're like a complete, obsessive lunatic. . . ."

"Laugh if you will, Ange," I said, "but you have to understand that a relationship is like a shark, because sharks swim and they have to eat a lot, and they're, like, underwater. . . ."

Or whatever. The important thing was, I treasured my relationship with Alphonse, and I wasn't about to let it all crumble. So I did what any conscientious pet owner would do, I took him to see Dr. Monique LaFarge, a leading pet psychologist I'd read about in one of our more reputable supermarket tabloids.

Dr. LaFarge was a formidable-looking woman, stout and fiercely tailored, with her hair in a bun and her reading glasses dangling round her neck on a cord. I could tell, by the way Alphonse clawed frantically at the door of his carrier when he saw her, that he was dubious about the benefits of therapy. Just like him to be so closed.

"Has Alphonse exhibited any unusual feline behavior?" the pet shrink asked as she ushered us into her office.

"He bolts out of a deep sleep and dashes around like a maniac," I answered. "He stares at a blank wall for hours. He hisses and hides behind a chair every time McGruff the Crime Dog comes on TV."

"So," she said, "nothing unusual."

"Not that I've noticed," I replied.

Then she asked me to wait outside while she consulted with Alphonse in private.

Dr. LaFarge was alone with Alphonse for twenty minutes before she called me in. Her office decor was a subtle blend of natural woods and earth tones. Above her desk was a painting of dogs playing poker. The dealer, I noticed, was a basset hound who looked like Freud.

Alphonse was sitting on his haunches in a comfy upholstered chair, staring at a wall chart showing a silhouette of a cat's head, and the compact brain within.

"Before I give you my diagnosis," said the pet shrink, "I want you to look at this diagram of the feline brain, which, as you can see, is divided into three distinct regions. The first lobe—comprising approximately forty percent of the feline gray matter—is devoted entirely to pondering the vital Can I eat it?/Can it eat me? conundrum. About fifteen percent is dedicated to meditating upon the crucial question Have I slept enough today? And the rest of the brain, of course, is set up to recognize can opener noises."

Alphonse absorbed the input with feline composure, then lifted his right rear leg and suavely licked his furry little gadget.

"But biology is only a small part of the cat's persona," said Dr. LaFarge. "Alphonse is obviously a complicated little fellow, with delicate sensibilities and a deep inner life. I think we may have some trust issues here. I think we need to rebuild his faith in you. So, I want you to buy him a case of gourmet cat food."

"Easy enough," I answered.

"And I want you to feed it to him, with a spoon."

"A spoon?"

"Yes," said the pet shrink. "In bed."

"He doesn't have a bed," I told her.

"No," she said. "In your bed. And sing to him while he eats."

"Sing to him?"

"Some Puccini," she said. "In a falsetto voice. Cats find falsetto very soothing."

Then she relieved me of seventy-five bucks and sent us on our way.

Dutifully, I drove Alphonse to the pet store to pick up the cat food. But once inside the store, a rebellious impulse struck me, and I veered over to the toys-and-accessories aisle where I scored a big bag of primo catnip. Then we went straight home, where I lit the lava lamp, put on some eight tracks from my countercultural college days (a little Cat Stevens, a little Hot Tuna), and Alphonse and I got mellow on some very tasty herb. (Well, I got mellow. Alphonse just snuffled his nose in the stuff, then wiggled around on his back like a demented June Taylor dancer.)

About ten minutes later, Al sat up and started to

make a heaving, snorkling noise like a sink drain with a suction problem. Then with a hoarse squeal, he coughed up a wad of compacted fur the size of a young avocado.

Instantly, a look of deep relief crossed his face, then he leapt onto my lap and started to purr. He was his sweet old self once again. I realized that we hadn't been drifting apart at all! Alphonse was simply stuffed to the gills with a ferocious hair ball!

So I opened a can of anchovies to celebrate, which led to some furious lip smacking and paw licking and rolling around on the floor. Bad table manners, to be certain, but what can I say? I love anchovies.

20
The Miracle Worker

I was out for a walk one morning when I spotted Nick on the street, having a snack at a Middle Eastern lunch cart. Stealthily, I crept up behind him, smacked him playfully between the angel bones, and spread my arms for a hug. But Nick didn't hug me. Instead, he put his hands to his throat, staggered down the sidewalk, and worked his mouth silently, like a carp.

I sized up the situation immediately—he had a chunk of falafel wedged in his gullet.

"Heimlich!" I shouted, to the throng of passersby. "Heimlich! Stand clear!"

Time was of the essence. I wrapped my arms around Nick's waist, balled my fists under his rib cage, and gave a quick, powerful squeeze, which dislodged the jammed morsel and lobbed it, like a mortar round, onto the hood of a passing taxi. When Nick stopped gasping, I led him off to a nearby coffeehouse, and fed him double lattes until he came around.

"You haven't returned my phone calls," I said as the color returned to his face.

"Didn't you get my message?" answered Nick. "I thought I spelled things out rather clearly—no more sessions until you finish the work on my house."

"I didn't think you meant that literally."

"I'm drawing the line," he said.

"But the work is going so well."

"It's not going well, Vinnie. You were supposed to fix a simple patch of damaged plaster, but the project keeps expanding. Now my whole house is in ruins."

"It's the chain of handiness, Doc." I shrugged. "One thing leads to another. . . ."

"Why did you tear up the floor in the bathroom?"

"You have old rusty galvanized pipes under there, Doc," I explained. "Didn't you ever notice the rust stains in your sink? It's only a matter of time until all those pipes start leaking, so it makes no sense to cover them up with fresh new plaster."

"But I can't get to the toilet."

"And you don't want to," I said. "While I was working on the galvy pipes, I got a look at your toilet drain— a big, creaky old cast-iron monstrosity seeping waste water at all the joints. That's why I ripped the rest of the plaster from the walls—makes it easier to run the new plastic drain lines."

Nick shook his head in agitation as the lattes arrived. "Don't you see what you're doing, Vinnie—you're venting all your handy urges at my expense."

"I know," I said, sipping the frothy java. "I'm really sold on this therapy thing."

"That's not the way it's supposed to work," muttered Nick.

"Who cares how it's supposed to work?" I said. "It's *working*. I'm getting my handy jollies at your place, which allows me to be the portrait of self-restraint at home. Ange is so pleased with my behavior, in fact, that she's very close to lifting her no-tools sanctions—I can be handy again! So, tell me I'm not getting my money's worth."

"I'd like to be alone," said Nick, staring out the window.

"No can do, Doc," I said. "I'm not leaving until I ask you about a dream."

"No," said Nick, "no therapy until you finish my house."

"But it's driving me crazy," I pleaded. "I can't sleep. I can't concentrate. . . ."

Nick waved his hand in the air. "Not my problem anymore," he said.

He seemed adamant. Clearly, I had to strike a deal. "Okay," I said, "here's my offer: Tell me what you think of the dream, and I promise, I'll finish your house by the end of the month."

"Will you put that in writing?" Nick asked.

I yanked a napkin from the tabletop dispenser and scribbled out the terms of a simple but binding contract. "There you go," I said. "Now, if I don't finish up by the thirty-first, you can take me to court."

"Oh, I won't sue you," said Nick as he folded the napkin and slipped it in his pocket. "I'll just tell Angela all about your little handy action on the side."

"You wouldn't do that," I gasped.

"In a minute," said Nick.

"What about doctor-patient confidentiality?" I pleaded. "You could lose your license."

"I'll take my chances," he snapped.

I really had no choice. "Deal," I said.

Nick nodded. "Okay. Let's hear the dream."

"It's a weird one," I said. "Ange and I come home from a trip and find our basement flooded. It's a regular lagoon down there. All our stuff is floating around like flotsam from a shipwreck. Old photographs, souvenirs, my catcher's mitt from Little League. And our traumatized cat, Alphonse, has been rafting for days in a Styrofoam ice bucket.

"I don't know why," I went on, "but the dream fills me with anxiety and dread. What do you think it means?"

Nick looked out the window as he thoughtfully sipped his latte. "Your dream is full of images of memory and nostalgia," he said. "I believe it indicates a deep personal issue you've long neglected, something emotional, something deep, which is now threatening to explode and inundate you, and overwhelm you in its turbulent flow."

"Bingo!" I whispered as I smacked myself on the forehead. "It's the water heater! Why didn't I see that? I've been neglecting that baby for years! It could blow at any moment.

"Doc," I cried, "you're a genius!" But Nick didn't gloat. Instead, he just groaned softly and let his head fall softly against the window.

"I'll be back in no time," I said. Then I flagged the waitress and pointed at Nick. "Lattes," I said, "and keep 'em coming!"

While driving home, I marveled at Nick's insightful perception. Modern hot water heaters are durable, efficient wonders that require only minimal attention from the homeowner. Perform a few minor maintenance chores from time to time, and your water heater will provide years of trouble-free service. Ignore those chores, however, and you could be asking for a steaming, indoor flash flood.

How do you keep your water heater happy? Start by understanding how it works. Basically, it's a big, simple holding tank. Cold water flows in, is warmed by a heat source in the tank's base, and then flows out through your plumbing to all the hot water faucets in your house.

What can go wrong? Leaks, for starters. Even the tiniest dribbles are harbingers of a watery cataclysm to come. Be vigilant. Check the heater's metal shell for signs of seepage, and look for leaks and corrosion where the cold water intake pipe, and the hot water exit pipe, join the tank. If you find signs of trouble, don't mess with repairs. Replace the tank as soon as you can.

No leaks? Excellent. Let's proceed to safety check number two, in which we make sure your water is not being heated hot enough to boil lobster. All you need to do is find the thermostat dial, mounted on the tank, which allows you to adjust the water temperature. Don't go below 110 degrees—that's the minimum for sanitary considerations—but keep in mind that anything higher than 120 degrees can scald. (Dishwashers sometimes call for 140-degree water, but you can usually get by with less. Or, you can find a dishwasher with its own water-heating unit.)

Okay, we've guarded against insidious leaks and random scaldings. Now let's check the device that should keep your tank from blowing up like a big, wet hand grenade.

The gizmo in question is called the pressure/temperature relief valve, a brass fitting with some sort of lever arm attached, implanted in the tank's flat top, or on the sidewall within six inches of the top. The purpose of this handy gizmo is to sense and safely vent off dangerous levels of temperature or pressure inside the tank.

If the pressure climbs too high, for example, it will spill enough water to bring things back in line, and if the temperature soars, the valve will vent a blast of steam until things settle down. (To prevent injury to bystanders, the P/T valve should be attached to a drainpipe that diverts hot water or steam safely down to the floor.)

The P/T valve is essential to the safe operation of your water heater, so you should check it every month to make sure it's in working order. It's an easy job, but remember, you'll be dealing with very hot water.

First, place a shallow pan on the floor beneath the valve's drainpipe, then lift the lever to trip the valve. Water should splash freely into the pan as long as you hold the valve open, and it should shut off completely as soon as the valve is closed. Any glitches mean the valve is faulty and should be cleaned or replaced. (If you've never done this before, consult a professional.)

Speaking of which, if you have an oil- or gas-fired water heater, you should call in a pro once a year to make sure the unit's vents and exhaust pipes are working properly. You don't want those nasty fumes and gases coming to find you when you're asleep.

Okay, those simple chores will keep your water heater safe. Now here's a bit of preventive maintenance that will boost its efficiency and add years to its life.

It has to do with sediment, stuff in the water that settles down to the bottom of the tank. Over time, sediment can build up into a layer thick enough to actually insulate the water from the heat source below. This forces the heater to work harder to warm the water, which results in higher utility bills and a shorter lifespan for the unit.

Fortunately, the fix is simple. See that threaded faucet nozzle down at the bottom of the tank? That's the drain valve. Just hook a garden hose to the faucet, open the valve, and drain off a few gallons of water into a nearby sink or floor drain (or out a window if you have to). This will siphon off most of the nasty sediment, and give your tank a new lease on life. Repeat this task every few months and your heater could not feel sweeter.

It took me less than an hour to perform all these routine maintenance chores on my own water heater. Then I raced back to the coffee house, where I found Nick still slumped at the table, mindlessly nibbling biscotti.

"I have to tell you, Nick," I said. "I feel great. Like a burden's been lifted from my soul. You're a miracle worker. I want to start seeing you again right now. Once a week. No, twice a week. Twice a week and maybe I stop over your place on weekends. I'll bring snacks. We can watch football. Say, do you like Parchesi?"

Nick didn't move a muscle. Barely even blinked. And I liked that, you know, realizing our relationship had grown to the point where we could be so comfortably silent together.

21
Farewell, Dino

he sky? Leaden. The wind? Bitter cold. Yours truly? Lost in a spiral of melancholia so deep not even the healing balm of handiness could cheer me.

It's true. I'd surrendered to despair. I'd lost my handy way. I had no stomach for tools or projects. My heart was empty, And my mind, where handy schemes once buzzed like beetles roasting on a bug zapper, was as bland and indolent as a boiled spud.

A bleak day. A day of grim tidings. I heard it first on CNN: Dean Martin, the crooning *paesano* with the gleaming black hair, frolics no more. Respiratory failure claims him. The world becomes a colder, less swinging place.

Immediately, I went into seclusion, in order to

properly grieve for the bleary-eyed Dino, the king of mock-tipsiness, the champion of halfhearted skirt chasers everywhere. I wrapped myself in my ratty old robe and collapsed on the sofa. I did not shave or shower for days. It was all I could do to muster the energy to rip open another Twinkies twin pack, or hit the rewind button on the VCR remote, as I wept through *Rio Bravo* over and over again.

At some point in this spiral of gloom, the telephone tweedled. I ignored it with a sigh and let the machine pick up the call. It was Nick. He sounded upset.

"Thought we were meeting today," he said. "Wondering why you didn't show. Lots of work to do, as you know. Need to nail things down. Tidy things up. Pull all the pieces together. Work toward closure. Sooner the better. You know what I mean. So please call me and tell me when you'll be by."

When he hung up, I hit the erase button and flopped back down on the couch. Hated to put Nick off, but I was much too depressed to talk with my shrink.

Just then, Ange walked in.

"Vinnie," she said. "It's three o'clock in the afternoon. Go take a shower."

"What's the point?" I morosely mumbled.

"The point is, you're disgusting," she said. "Look at you: Your lips are smeared with double-fudge icing, you have Fritos crumbs in your hair, there's dried Ovaltine dribble all down your chin. . . ."

"Who cares?" I muttered as I gobbled up a cream-filled chocolate cupcake. "It's all pointless, anyway."

"I care," snapped Angie. "You're ruining my new couch."

"Please, Ange," I said, gesturing toward the TV, "a little respect for the grieving."

Ange brushed some Pizzarino crumbs off the sofa and carefully sat down. "I know you're upset about Dino," she said, taking my hands in hers, "but you have to accept this; it was his time."

Time, indeed. I heaved a heavy sigh and stared at the ceiling. Oh Dino, Dino, Dino. Where have they gone, those golden Rat Pack days of dames, smokes, convertibles, highballs, fistfights, shiny suits, and snappy manly banter? Back then guys had stand-up buddies; you pulled capers, you drank bourbon, you had dinner in clubs at midnight, you played poker until dawn. Now, everyone is always on-line, or they're screening their calls, or they're not drinking these days except for a little white wine, or they can't meet you at the Sands for the 1 A.M. show, but maybe they can squeeze you in for a decaf latte at Starbuck's unless little Jurgen's soccer game runs long.

"Tell you what," said Ange, "I can see you need some cheering up. And since you've been so well behaved lately, handy-wise, why don't I let you go down to the root cellar and visit your tools?"

I grunted unenthusiastically and opened a bag of barbecue-style Corn Nuts.

"Come on, Vinnie, your tools," she cajoled. "I'll let you take them out and clean them if you want."

"Leave me alone," I mumbled.

"But Vinnie, your tools . . ."

"I don't care about my tools," I moped. "I don't care about anything. I don't want to be handy anymore."

Angie's eyes widened as she sensed I meant what I said. "Are you serious?" she said. "No more urge to fix?"

I nodded, numbly. "Your wish has finally come true."

"No more walls tumbling?" she said, "No more holes in the roof? No more torn-up floors . . . ?"

I gave her a sarcastic grin and popped open a can of savory Vienna sausages.

"No more angry neighborhood petitions?" she continued. "No more surprise inspections from the ATF?"

"You don't have to rub it in," I said.

"But if you don't fix things," said Angie, "what will you do?"

I shifted among the crinkling litter of snack cake wrappers and empty Cheetos bags, in my rumpled, sweaty pj's, and settled more deeply into the billowy cushions of her new designer couch. Then I spread my arms and answered, "This."

Ange chuckled softly, then her face grew troubled and drawn. "You're starting to scare me," she said.

I dodged the comment with a frown and rubbed my itchy nose against the sofa's nubbly brocade.

Ange suddenly rose to her feet and clapped her hands lightly, like somebody calling a dog.

"Come on, Vincent," she coaxed. "Up on your feet and let me see you fix something, okay?"

When I didn't budge, Ange rushed from the room. She returned, moments later, with a wobbly kitchen chair.

"This is dangerous," she said. "Get your tools out and fix it."

I burped on Dr Pepper and stuffed another Moon Pie down my gullet.

Ange dashed off to the basement and came back with a fractured picture frame. "I need this," she said. "How about patching it together?"

I shook my head and scratched myself extravagantly.

But Ange wouldn't quit. For the next half hour, she rummaged through the basement, the attic, the closets, and all the drawers, searching for a handy project with which to lure me from the doldrums. She brought cracked vases, broken mirrors, lopsided end tables, and lamps with fraying chords. None of it moved me. I only sank deeper into woe.

Then Ange came down from the second floor with a curious smile on her face. She knelt beside the couch and whispered in my ear: "Vincent, there's an emergency in the bathroom. I think the toilet's leaking."

I groaned and hid my face with a couch cushion.

"Oh come on, Vinnie," she cooed. "Do it for me. You know how it gets to me when you do plumbing."

That, I couldn't let pass. "You hate it when I do plumbing," I said.

"Oh, no," she replied. "I find it very erotic. Maybe it

seems like I hate it, because I'm a little frightened by the depth of passion it inspires. I mean, plungers, P traps, plumber's putty . . ."

I felt a small but definite stirring of desire.

"This comes as something of a surprise," I admitted.

"It shouldn't," she cooed. "Don't you remember our honeymoon cabin on the coast of Maine? The one with the big stone fireplace, in the tall pines, with the beautiful view of the rocky cove."

"The one where I burned down the kitchen?" I reminisced.

"That was an honest mistake," she said.

"At the time," I replied, "you seemed very angry."

"Oh, no," she said with a soft, seductive laugh.

"You threw a dish at me," I pointed out. "You made me sleep in the woods, on a hammock."

"I was a kid," Ange explained. "What did I know about love?"

"You wouldn't let me see you naked for the rest of the trip."

"My emotions were so strong," she said, "it was all so overwhelming."

"Really?"

"Oh, yeah," Angie purred. "Don't get a big head, now, but you should know, you're quite breathtaking when you work with pipes and wrenches."

Fascinating, isn't it, the mystery of attraction? I couldn't help wondering, was it the way I handled the shiny pipes in my strong capable hands, or the manly can-do aura that is a natural attribute of a man well versed in the plumbing arts? Or, could it be as simple as the promise made by a fleeting glimpse of tastefully tantalizing butt cleavage?

"Let's don't analyze," Ange replied when I put the question to her. "We might spoil the magic. Why don't you just go on up and attend to the toilet. You'll feel a lot better if you fix something."

I smiled sadly. "I couldn't do that," I said.

"Why not?"

"I'm grieving," I said sighing.

Ange nodded. "What stage?" she said.

"Pardon?"

"What stage of grief? Bargaining? Denial?"

"I don't follow—"

"I think you're in Depression. That's stage four. Tough one. Know what's good for that?"

"Ice bath?" I guessed. "Mustard plaster? Mega-doses of Saint Johns Wort?"

Ange shook her head sagely. "Plumbing," she said.

I rolled away from Ange and burrowed back into the sofa. "I really don't have it in me." I sighed.

"Oh, it's in you," said the suddenly animated Ange as she hoisted me to my feet by the collar of my robe. "It's in you, toots, believe me."

My feet were barely touching the floor as she bum-rushed me up the stairs.

"What are you doing?" I said as she shoved me into the bathroom.

"You need a jump start," she answered. "You need a boot in the pants."

"But Ange," I whimpered, "I have no verve."

"Then get verve," Ange hissed. "I want you trembling with verve. I want you in a nice, familiar handy frenzy. I want you off my new sofa and out of this gloomy daze. I hate to do this, Babe, but I'm not letting you out of this bathroom until you fix that john."

Then she slammed the door and locked it from the outside, and then I was alone. Wearily, I sat on the edge of the bathtub and looked at the floor beneath the toilet. Water was pooled all around the porcelain base. I forced myself to consider the possible sources of the seepage. Maybe some connection in the supply line was leaking. Maybe the waterproof gasket between the tank and the bowl had failed. There was a slim chance that the innards of the bowl had cracked, and water was oozing out under the base of the commode. So many possible problems, it made me all sleepy and blue. Then, as my natural defenses kicked in, I curled up on the floor of the tub and sought the soothing refuge of slumber.

Moments later, I woke to girlish laughter. I opened my eyes and saw a leggy Vegas showgirl leaning against the sink. Next to her was Dino, in a swank gray dinner jacket with black-satin lapels. He was flashing that heavy-lidded, faux-boozy smile, and his shiny hair was perfect as he sang the showgirl a tune:

"Eerray bodd-ehhh loves som bodd-ehhh . . . sum dime. . . ."

It was magical. Then Dino spotted me in the tub. He raised the highball glass in a silent toast, took a sip, and mugged comically as the drink trickled down his chin.

"Okay," he said, feigning boozy anger, "who slipped me the dribble glass?" Then he raised the drink to the light. Beads of perspiration covered the outside of the glass.

"Lookee there," he said, in street accent. "I thinks we gots us a conden-SAY-tion problem. . . ."

Then he toasted me again and disappeared.

I woke from the dream with a start, instantly understanding the message Dino had sent to me in the dream. My toilet wasn't leaking, it was sweating.

Here's what happens, see: The cold water in your toilet tank cools the tank's outer surface. Then, when warm, moist, room air comes in contact with that cool porcelain surface, it condenses into drops, and the outside of the tank sweats like a highball glass in summer.

This dribbling dampness is not only sloppy and unpleasant, it also can drip to the floor and mildew your rugs or even seep down through seams in your floor coverings to ruin the wooden floor below. Fortunately, there are several simple ways to solve the problem.

First, you could fit the tank with one of those fuzzy, terry cloth tank covers. That will keep warm room air from striking the cool porcelain, hence, no condensation. And even if a few droplets do form, they'll be quickly blotted up by the cover's absorbent liner. These covers come in a range of unsettlingly garish colors, and while they may ruin your shot at a spread in *Metropolitan Home,* they'll provide a quick cheap fix for your sweaty toilet.

If, on the other hand, you'd like a toilet that makes less of a fashion statement, you can install an inexpensive tank liner kit. These kits consist of several sheets of rigid foam insulation and a special adhesive. You just cut the sheets to fit and glue them to the insides of the tank. The foam insulates the outside of the tank from the cool water inside, and, voilà, no sweaty toity.

It shouldn't take longer than an hour to install one of these kits. It's the kind of job I used to knock off during commercial breaks while watching the Judge Judy show. But today, I didn't have the heart to even get started, so I curled up in the tub again and drifted off to dreamland. Moments later, I heard Ange unlocking the door.

"Vincent," she said, "there's someone here to see you."

I looked up and there was Dr. Nick, looking so cheery it concerned me.

"House calls, Doc?" I grumbled.

"Angela thinks we should talk," he said.

"I'll leave you two alone," said Angie. "If you want me, I'll be down in the living room, shampooing the couch."

Nick smiled until Angela disappeared through the doorway, then he bent down to tub level and hissed in an agitated whisper, "What does she mean, you don't want to be handy anymore? You're going to be plenty handy, pal. You have to put my office back together."

I shrugged balefully. "Handyness requires such optimism," I whimpered, "such energy, such faith. I just don't have it in me anymore."

"But what about my house?" said Nick. "There's a six-foot stack of two-by- fours in my dining room. Every inch of the place is covered in dust. I have no walls, no ceiling. And why did you board up the windows with plywood?"

"With all the work we're doing, it only made sense to rip out those drafty old casements and put in some snug new triple-paned beauties. I have the new windows on order. They'll be here in a week or two."

"You were just supposed to patch some plaster."

"Who knows where the chain of handiness might lead?"

"You have to finish now!" he screamed. "Last night, I had a session with my obsessive-compulsive group. These guys won't even touch a public doorknob. When they saw the mess in my office, three of them had to be sedated."

"I want to help, Doc," I said, "but I just feel so blue."

"Well we're going to cheer you up now," said Nick, fumbling through his pockets until he found a plastic vial. His hands were trembling as he twisted off the cap and shook some yellow pills into his hand. "Take these," he snapped.

"I thought you didn't like dishing out pills—"

"Just take them! Get happy! Get happy, now!"

I popped a pill in my mouth and smiled. When Nick turned away, I used a technique I'd learned from my cat, Alphonse, and tongue-whipped the pill across the room.

"All right, Vinnie," said Nick as he handed me a manila envelope. "I had hoped it wouldn't come to this."

Inside the envelope were candid Polaroids of me working at Nick's house. The piles of plaster rubble looked much higher on film.

"You took pictures?" I said.

"I like this one," said Nick, holding up one of the snapshots. "I like the way the camera catches the sledge-hammer just as it splinters my bedroom wall. This is a prize winner," he said. "Let's go show Ange."

"You wouldn't," I whispered.

"Maybe she'd like this one better," Nick suggested as he showed me a shot of yours truly dancing like Rocky Balboa atop a mound of fallen plaster.

I took the pills from Nick with a smile of resignation.

"Mmmm," I said as I gobbled them down, "tastes a little like Pez."

22
A Night to Remember

As weeks passed, I struggled hard to finish all the work at Nick's, but that was easier said than done. Could I close up a wall, for example, in which an active leak existed? Could I, in good conscience, reconnect the tub and toilet to supply lines I knew were going to fail? And could I pass up the golden opportunity to drop in a nice new skylight in Dr. Nick's bedroom, even if it meant slicing a big ragged hole in his roof?

My point is, things had to get worse before they got better. To me that was clear. Nick, on the other hand, had trouble grasping the vision, and he wasn't handling the handy pressures very well. He grew increasingly anxious and withdrawn. In our sessions, his insights lost their oomph. (I'd bare my soul concerning some inner pain, or hopeless longing, for example, and he'd mumble, "Yeah, whatever.")

He began canceling appointments for unconvincing reasons. (A broken cup-holder in your Volvo, for example, is not a legitimate excuse for skipping work.) I began to spot him hanging out in dark corners of shadowy cafés, wearing sunglasses at nighttime, but by the time I'd make way to his table he'd have silently slipped away.

I was worried. I tried not to make too much of it, but soon I'd begun to wonder if I'd come on too strong with Nick. Perhaps, I pondered, I was crowding him with my raging handy needs. So, to be thoughtful, I stocked the El Camino with Cheetos and a tub of hot java, grabbed my infrared night-vision goggles, and put his house under round-the-clock surveillance, hoping to spot him and ask him if he needed some space.

But Nick never showed. The last time I called his number, someone speaking in a faltering Balkan accent assured me, "Ve haff no Neek here vhatsoeffer. Please to not be calling us, at all."

Then the line went dead. After that, my calls all went unanswered. He had dumped me. He had hit the road. When the truth struck home, I realized fully how deeply I depended on Nick. I mean, not only was he my trusted counselor, and a shining beacon in the dark and stormy harbor of handy confusion that was my life, he was also providing me with the only opportunity I had to vent the explosive do-it-yourself urges that simmer inside me. With Nick gone, those frustrated handy urges began to surge and rumble, and no good ever comes of that. I was in full-blown handy withdrawal. My bones ached, my skin crawled. My ranch-flavored Pizzarino consumption was off the charts.

I was in misery, but I struggled to hide it all from Ange, poor kid, who was pleased as punch at what she saw as my dramatic improvement. After all, as far as she knew, I hadn't touched a tool in months. She had no idea I was getting my handy desires satisfied outside the marriage.

God, I felt like such a crumb, but such was the power of my addiction that I couldn't help myself. I had to have a handy fix. So, one night, I treated Ange to a lavish candlelight dinner.

"Ange," I said as I helped her to her seat and filled her glass with wine, "I want to make this a night to remember."

Ange tipped the glass to her lips and drank slowly. Then she set the glass on the table and gave me a challenging stare. "What did you have in mind?" she cooed.

"I'm planning something big," I said. "Something bold, something reckless, something a little bit dangerous."

"I'm very intrigued," answered Ange.

"It'll be emotional and impulsive," I told her. "It'll shake the foundations of the house."

"Promises, promises," Angie said sighing.

"It'll be sweaty and noisy," I said. "The neighbors

might call the cops. It'll take days for the dust to settle."

Angie batted her long, dark lashes. "Talk is cheap," she muttered.

She was daring me! She was game! I didn't want to waste another minute.

"Let's get started," I cried, lurching from my seat. "You spread the canvas tarps, I'll set up the floodlights."

Angie recoiled slightly as her face scrunched up in puzzlement, then a look of recognition flashed in her dark Sicilian eyes.

"You're talking about knocking down a wall, aren't you?" she muttered.

I smiled and cocked my head sheepishly. "Small wall," I muttered. "Partial wall, maybe. . . ."

Ange nodded calmly as she knitted her fingers together and smiled that sweet, bloodcurdling smile.

"Basement?" I inquired.

"Sweet dreams," said she.

And so I found myself, once again, languishing down under. I guess Ange will never understand my passion for this particular home improvement project. As far as I'm concerned, in all of handidom, there's no more satisfying thrill than the ritual demolition of an old plaster wall. My method is to stand reverently before the doomed wall like an Oglala Sioux about to finish off a downed bison. I gather myself into a meditative state, then when the moment's right, I drop into a Sumo squat, raise my crowbar above my head, and duckwalk forward into the fray.

I swing the crowbar so hard that the curved claw pierces the hard plaster and hooks into the wooden lath below. Then I give a mighty tug, and the wall explodes like a Claymore mine, sending plaster rubble and splintered chunks of lath swirling all around me. Dust clouds billow. Pebbles of plaster doink off my brow. But I keep swinging until the walls are stripped down to the skeletal studs and my autonomic nervous system is abuzz with primal, prevertebrate joy.

And when it's over, there is space and light and nasty black stuff in my phlegm for days.

You too can feel this heady sense of power, but unless, like me, you hold a black belt in the handy arts, I urge you to pursue things in a more cautious fashion. Before laying a hand on the targeted wall, for example, have a structural engineer determine if the wall is carrying a structural load. Structural "bearing walls" can be removed, but the project requires sophisticated engineering and carpentry techniques, and since any mistake might topple your house, it's a job best left to the pros. On the other hand, "partition walls," which separate living spaces but carry no loads, can usually be knocked out without any structural concerns.

Also, carefully consider how removing the wall will change your living space. It'll add more room and light, sure, but it might also alter traffic patterns in a way that could deprive you of privacy, make for a noisier house, and leave you with an awkwardly proportioned space that's impossible to decorate and furnish.

The way around all this, of course, it to carefully plot things out. Take careful measurements of the rooms involved and sketch the new space, to scale, on graph paper. Measure your furniture too, and draw it in. Experiment with different arrangements. And don't raise a hand to that wall until you're sure the new space you're creating is an improvement over what you have.

Also, be advised that you'll need to reroute any pipes, ducts, and electrical cables you discover inside the wall. That'll be easy when the wall is open, but for safety's sake, you might want to shut off the electrical power while you work.

Okay, consider yourself forewarned. Now, don the hard hat, the work gloves, the dust mask, and the protective eyewear. Be serious with your safety gear, 'cause this won't be no disco.

I won't kid you, downing a plaster wall is a dusty, grimy endeavor, but I'm going to show you an approach that keeps the environmental mayhem to a minimum. The first step is to scrupulously prepare the site. After clearing the area, tape plastic tarps across the doorways to contain the rolling dust clouds. Drape more plastic over windows, mantels, bookcases, and so on. (If it's a small room, you can cut your postproject cleanup considerably by taping thin plastic sheets over all the walls.)

Use heavier cloth tarps, taped at the edges, to protect a carpeted floor; and shield wood floors with cardboard sheets laid under the tarps. Now gather your tools—a hammer, a crowbar, and a hunk of a two-by-four about twelve inches long—and prepare to par-tay. But first, a brief lesson in wall anatomy.

Vertical studs—two-by-fours or two-by-sixes stood on end—form the structural skeleton of your wall. If the wall is covered in drywall sheets, the sheets are simply nailed or screwed to the studs. Not much to removing drywall—you smash it with the claw of your hammer, and pull it off in big chunks. To remove a plaster wall with minimal mayhem, you must loosen the tireless grasp of the keys.

That's where the two-by-four comes in. I want you to lay it flat against the wall and give it a respectable whack with the hammer. The two-by-four will spread the force of the blow, sending shock waves through the plaster that should cause those brittle keys to crumble. No need to go Neanderthal, here; no need to smash the wall into crumbly bits. Just swing hard enough to cause a maze of hairline cracks.

Now, slide the two-by-four across the wall as you whack it. You'll hear the keys rattling inside the wall as they snap off and tumble, and you'll feel the plaster sagging and cracking into sizeable plates. When you've worked over a section of the wall, use the claw of your hammer to carefully pry off chunks of the plaster, or just pull them free with your hand. Most of the plaster should come off without a struggle, but if you hit any stubborn sections, a few light taps with the side of your hammer should loosen things up.

As you pry off the plaster, piece by piece, drop it into cardboard boxes lined with garbage bags. (Don't overfill the boxes; this stuff is heavy.)

When all the plaster has been stripped off, boxed, and hauled clear, it's time to make war on the lath boards. These are tough, ornery little strips of wood, springy and brittle, and studded with rusty nails. Approach them with caution and respect.

The best way to remove the lath is to yank on them with the crowbar, at the point where the end of each lath board meets a stud. Just pop the nails free.

When the lath is down, gather it in bundles and tie it up with string. (Removing the lath and plaster separately eliminates those harrowing piles of rubble and splintered wood, and makes cleanup much easier.)

With the plaster and lath removed, the anatomy of the wall reveals itself: The vertical studs, spaced sixteen or twenty-four inches apart, are nailed, at the ceiling and the floor, to long horizontal members known as "plates."

The easiest way to remove a stud is to saw through its midpoint, then wiggle each half back and forth like a lever, until the nails holding it to its respective plate work free.

Removing the plates, which are stoutly nailed to the frame of the house, requires a little more effort. I like to use a nail-pulling pry bar called a "cat's paw" to yank out as many nails as I can. Then I use the pry bar's flat blade to pry the piece free. (Get some help with that top plate so it doesn't drop on your noggin.)

When the demolition's done and the dust has cleared, there'll be light and space and plaster grit in your teeth, and you'll never in your life feel more gloriously handy.

And in my mind, I was standing proud atop a pile of fallen plaster, basking in that handy glory, when Ange appeared at the bottom of the cellar steps.

"I've been thinking," she said. "This evening started off so well, it doesn't have to be a total loss."

It seemed prudent at that point to hold my tongue.

"I mean, even if you don't knock down a wall," she said, "there's still plenty of time for other sorts of noisy, sweaty fun."

"There is?" I answered, my voice sounding like I'd just sucked on a helium balloon.

"We have all night," whispered Angie.

"Sweaty, noisy fun?"

"Sweaty, noisy, dusty, and very, very handy," she said.

"Mercy," I said, fanning myself.

"I plan to keep you busy . . . ," said Ange.

"Good," I said. "I'm goal oriented."

"Can you last until daybreak?" she challenged.

Yikes, pressure. "When you say 'last' . . . ," I gingerly inquired.

"How about supplies?" she interrupted. "Are we covered?"

I didn't follow. "You mean, like scented candles? Massage oil? Ostrich feathers?"

Angie chuckled. "I mean, like plaster of Paris, and weatherproof glue," she replied.

"Ange," I snickered, "you kinky minx."

Then my luminously beautiful wife just smiled at me until I caught the drift.

"We're talking about the gnomes, " I surmised.

"I want ten finished by morning," she said. "You promised Mrs. Plumpton you'd have them back in her yard by Christmas. You're falling way behind."

Then Ange climbed the stairs, and once again I was alone with the despicable throng of plaster trolls. That night I found them particularly repulsive. One of them—the chubby-cheeked winking one who looked like a half-pint Ed Asner—was really getting to me. So I went right up and got in his face and told him, Keep it up, chump, because I have tools handy and I'm still in the mood to bust up some plaster.

23
Pests

ow long had I languished in my gnome-infested basement exile? I'd lost track, to tell you the truth. Ange wasn't speaking to me. Nick was nowhere to be found. I was exiled and alone, and like many a hopeless dungeon dweller in less enlightened days of yore, I was scratching out the passing days on the cold stone walls of my prison, darkly nursing my grievances, wondering what to do with the bitterness simmering in my soul.

Then I spotted the tunnels: skinny termite mud tunnels snaking up my foundation wall toward a big juicy beam. The pulpy little wood-munching devils had invaded, and were snacking on the very structural backbone of my house.

I could imagine them, in their teeming thousands,

nibbling gleefully on my lumber. Eager. Remorseless. Insatiable. What did they care if my charming little bungalow tumbled around my ears, the wiggling little sociopaths.

It was the ultimate insult. Their arrogant disregard made my blood boil.

I stared at the beam for long, dark moments, imagining the squirming intruders inside. I could almost hear the relentless greedy gnoshing, the tinny little insect cries of glee. I vowed to make them pay.

So I smiled an evil smile and whispered, in a voice I knew they could hear, "I love the smell of chlordane in the morning. It smells like victory!"

Chlordane, for those of you not up to speed on toxic household chemicals, is one of the most powerful agents in the pest-fighter's arsenal. Of course, I had to have some, but that's easier said than done. Chlordane can't be sold to the civilian public, and despite my constant lobbying, the feds still stubbornly refuse to consider my application for Special Agent status. (Not really interested in espionage, mind you, but I think it would be a great way to lay my hands on some very handy hardware. For example, take those smart bombs that can find their way down a skinny ventilation shaft. Imagine what short work they'd make of a bad sewer clog.)

Anyway, there was no legal way to procure the chemical, so I did what any sensible ultrahandyman would do: I waited through the night, and when Ange had left for work in the morning I disguised my voice and called the local chemical supply house.

"Aye, lassie," I said, "and a bonnie good day to ya! Could you be sending over some lawn fertilizer, some pH chemicals for me pool, some bagpipe oil, and a wee jug o' your finest chlordane?"

There was silence on the line. "I know you," she said. "You've called before."

"Oh no, lassie . . ." I chuckled. "'Tis a first-time caller I am. Haggis is my name. Haggis McKorckle."

"Huh-uh," she said. "You're the guy who tried to buy the nerve agent for your gopher problem. Jimmy!" she cried out. "It's the nerve agent guy!"

"Calm down," I said, scrapping the accent. "I'll level with you. Truth is . . . I'm the governor, and I need your help in a matter of great urgency. . . ."

I heard someone whisper in the background, "I've got three numbers; keep him talking," so I slammed down the receiver before they could make the trace. I could almost hear the termites tittering. I had no choice; I had to call for professional help.

An hour later Larry the exterminator knocked on my door. Dressed in crisp, paramilitary khakis, with a ramrod posture and an assassin's calculating stare, he was a portrait of fierce dignity and steely resolve (if you overlooked the big plastic cockroach on the roof of his van).

In any case, he seemed to be just the guy to rain righteous doom upon those six-legged gluttons who were devouring my house.

I showed Larry the beam. He poked it with a screwdriver, shined his flashlight all around, then gave me the word.

"No serious damage," he said. "We caught 'em just in time. You're very lucky. They'd have hollowed out that beam, and then you'd be looking at real trouble."

As Larry prepared to do battle, he smartened me up on termite ways. They live underground, he said, where the earth provides the moisture so crucial to their survival. But they surface every day to feed—they actually get nourishment from wood. Then the crafty beggars return to the nest each night, traveling through the little tunnels they build to protect themselves from exposure. But if the wood is moist enough to sustain them, they'll be happy to stay put and chow down around the clock.

Termites are found everywhere, except in the coldest northern latitudes, but they don't have a monopoly on the munching of houses. There are also carpenter ants to contend with. These ants don't actually eat the wood, they just hollow out chambers in which to make their nests.

And we can't forget powder post beetles, which can live their entire lives chomping inside a beam, then lay their eggs in the wood so that the gluttony continues generation after generation.

Carpenter ants are the least destructive, and you can treat them yourself, but before you disturb them, follow their trails until you find their nest, where the all-important queen ant resides. You must ice queenie. Then the disheartened colony will disperse. Over-the-counter pesticides will do the job.

Beetles and termites, meanwhile, require a higher level of chemical ordnance, which is available only to certified pros like Larry, who was already approaching my infested beam with a cool, murderous gleam in his eye. He was itching to pull the trigger, I could tell, but being a pro, he paused and said a few words about prevention.

The trick, he said, is to catch things early. Look for telltale mud tunnels on your foundation walls or on gas or water pipes that enter from outside. Watch for small oblong holes in wood, or drifts of fine sawdust, which might reveal the presence of powder post beetles. Periodically poke your joists and beams with a long screwdriver, to test for damaged wood. And call an exterminator if you see winged ants swarming, or find an accumulation of tiny insect wings, which termites rub off when they spawn.

Above all, Larry stressed the importance of common sense. All these lumber-munchers are attracted to moisture, he said, so you can discourage their arrival by keeping the wood of your house snug and dry. Make sure your attic and crawl spaces are well ventilated, patch any roof leaks and leaky pipes, and look for cracks and gaps in your exterior siding where water might seep in.

It also helps, he said, to be tidy. Don't leave lumber

or tree limbs lying on the ground near your house; that's like ringing the termite dinner bell. Likewise, don't store firewood against an exterior wall, and make sure, when you dig a new foundation, that no one buries wood scraps with the fill. If your house has wooden clapboards, be certain none of them come in contact with the ground. (You might as well roll down a gangplank and send out invitations.)

In my case, of course, those warnings had come too late, and now it was up to Larry to wreak havoc with whatever dazzling weapons he had at his command.

"So, how do we take them?" I asked. "Radioactive implants? Midget lasers? Tiny dots of plastique?"

"We spray them," said Larry, holding up a dumpy-looking little tank with a spray wand attached.

"That looks a little . . . dorky," I answered.

"This will do the job."

I was underwhelmed. "I want to hit them hard, Larry."

"They'll hate this," he said.

"I pictured something more aggressive."

"This is the standard treatment."

"How about some cobalt gas?"

"Could you step back, please?"

"Wait," I said, "I don't think you're catching my drift. I want catastrophe, here. I want annihilation. I want to rain some Bible-caliber wrath upon these bugs."

"Sir," said Larry, "I only spray."

I nodded and said, "I want a second opinion."

So I spoke with several other exterminators, and every one suggested the same approach. Then I met Armand, who, being new to the pest-purging industry (his professional roots are in meat-packing), was more open to innovation.

"I want extreme extermination," I said. "I want you to stretch a tarp over the house and pump it full of the most toxic substance you can get you hands on, *capice?*

"No problem," said Armand.

"You've done it before?"

"Well, no," he answered. "But I saw it on Bob Vila."

"Perfect," I said. "When can you start?"

"Soon as I find a tarp that big," he said.

A week later, Armand and his crew arrived and began stretching an ocean of rubber sheeting across the roof.

"It's an old helium balloon from the Thanksgiving parade," he said. "I patched it up; it's just the ticket."

When the tarp was lashed in place, Armand revved up his pump. It took a few million cubic feet of poison gas to inflate the balloon. Armand's crew had to rig up floodlights and labor into the night, and when they finished, my charming little bungalow had disappeared beneath the rubbery loins of a three-story cartoon chicken.

Unluckily, it was just as the chicken had reached full turgidity that Angie came home from her Oprah Winfrey book club. She glanced at the towering, floodlit chicken, crossed her arms, and looked at me.

"Why is there a gigantic Foghorn Leghorn squatting on our house?" she calmly inquired. But before I could reply, Armand approached with a clipboard.

"I did some calculations like you asked," he said. "And I figure, one week at the latest, the house will again be able to sustain human life."

I quickly complimented Ange on her new shoes, but it was too little, too late. Her face scrunched up into a furious grimace, and she began to mutter under her breath, so I beat feet out of there on the double, before she could whack me upside the head with her hardback copy of *Angela's Ashes*.

24
Wild-Man
Weekend

At first, sure, having a three-story cartoon chicken perched upon your house is exciting stuff. You have the tourists driving by. The papers all do stories. The local news teams can't get enough of you.

But soon, the glamour fades and the celebrity rings hollow and you are left to face a very definite downside—with that thick yellow fog of lethal pesticide fumes still billowing inside it, my house wouldn't be liveable for another three days. Ange had decamped to her mother's house to wait out the fumes. Conspicuously, she hadn't invited me to join her. Likewise, she wasn't returning my calls. So I decided to motor north into the mountains, to my little rustic cabin in the woods, where I'd hole up for a week or so until she came to her senses.

The getaway was just the tonic I needed. Out in

the forest primeval, I could throw myself into a handy frenzy without hurting anybody. And once my backed-up how-to urges had been safely burned off, maybe my head would clear enough to think about finding the wayward Nick and putting my life back together.

Fortunately I'd anticipated the need to travel, and before I let them fumigate my house I'd stocked the El Camino with all the provisions I needed to in order to go on the road. I had warm clothing and blankets, some freeze-dried field rations, a basic first aid kit, and of course, a nice selection of tools. I'd also filled a separate sack with a few random niceties, to give the rustic cabin some of the comforts of home—my favorite lava lamp, my Cisco Kid pajamas, my glow-in-the-dark travel bust of Elvis, and so on.

The cabin was five hours north, nestled on the rugged slope of a remote wooded ridge. The first thing I saw when I got there was that the shrubbery was out of control. It was late afternoon, and I had only a few hours of daylight left, but I was so anxious to get handy that I went to work before unpacking the car.

First, I surveyed the situation. The ornamental vegetation decorating the cabin's little yard had been sadly neglected, and that was a handy shame. Properly situated and cared for, bushes and trees can be hard-working additions to your property. They shield houses from damaging sunlight and wind, they shade yards and porches, and they add beauty to your home. On the other hand, neglected, they can do real damage.

For example, overhanging tree limbs can rub your roof shingles raw, clog your gutters with fallen leaves and needles, and give ballsy squirrels a springboard onto your roof and eventually into your attic, where they will nest, store nuts, and wreak all sorts of rodent mayhem, such as gnawing through the insulation of electrical wires, and maybe burning down your house.

How about the shrubs? Bushes planted too close to the house can prevent sunlight from reaching your exterior walls, restrict air circulation, and trap moisture—all of which can lead to the growth of wood-rotting fungus. And tall shrubs around windows and entrances can give burglars a comfy place to hide. So, spare not the pruning shears. Your rooted friends want you, they need you, to exercise control.

Which was just what I intended to do, but when I checked the little toolshed behind the cabin, I found that all my garden tools had rusted solid.

So I jumped back into the El Camino, knowing I could make it to the hardware store in the nearest town if I used the shortcut I'd discovered the last time I was here. So I cranked the engine and headed down a winding dirt road that led me deeper into the woods.

Maybe I was driving too fast. Maybe it was road fatigue, from being at the wheel all day. In any case, I didn't see the deer until I was right on top of her.

Instinctively, I swerved to miss her, which sent the El Camino plunging into a ravine. I remember my headlights flashing on the underbrush. I remember bouncing like a rodeo cowboy riding a Brahma bull. I remember that big fat tree trunk approaching. Then, all was quiet and dark.

When I opened my eyes, I found myself lying on my back in the underbrush. And I realized I wasn't alone. There were ten guys there, maybe twelve, standing around me in a circle. They were wearing animal pelts and feathered headdresses. They all had their faces painted. Some of them were holding spears.

The guy closest to me was a lanky fellow holding what looked like a big ceremonial baby's rattle, with peacock feathers and animal bones dangling from the handle.

"Speak, brother," he said when he saw I'd come around.

"Who are you?" I said, squinting in recognition of the throbbing pain in my noggin.

"I am Wolf, the shaman," he said, "and this is my warrior clan. We are the Wild Men of the Woods."

"What are you," I said, "some lost, wandering tribe, or something?"

"Actually," said a bare-chested chubby guy wearing a bear-tooth necklace and a tutu made from palm fronds, "we just do this on weekends. We're trying to recapture a sense of mythic manliness and reconnect with the Manly Iron Warrior inside."

"Oh," I said, "so you're not, like, a full-time wild man?"

The chubby guy shook his head. "I'm wild, like, twenty-five percent of the time, maybe," he said. "Otherwise, I manage the frozen yogurt place on Route Fifty-five. Tasty Licks?"

He took off his headdress, fished around in the band, then pulled out a wrinkled card and handed it to me. "It's a punch card," he said. "Buy five cones, get the sixth one free."

"Cougar," said the shaman, "do you mind?"

"Sorry," said Cougar as he nestled the headdress back on his balding head.

Now the shaman stared me down, coming off all ironlike. "Who are you, stranger," he demanded, "and why are you travelling alone, at night, through the woods?"

I gave the question a full thirty seconds of careful thought.

"Want to hear something interesting?" I said. "I don't have a clue." It was true. I wouldn't have known myself from Adam.

The shaman's eyes narrowed. "You don't know who you are?" he inquired.

"Couldn't even tell you what I look like," I confessed.

"And you remember nothing about the crash?"

My eyes widened as I looked at the wreckage behind me. "Is that my car?" I asked. "Geeze, am I all right?"

The shaman turned to his fellow wild men. "He seems to have no recollection, at all," he said.

I felt bad. I wanted to give him something. "I do remember bumping my head," I offered.

The shaman was silent for a moment. Then he motioned for the wild men to gather a few feet away. For a minute or two, they quietly conferred. Then they all turned to face me.

"You will come to our encampment and spend the night," he declared. "In the morning, Eagle here will lead you to a nearby village. Until then, you are part of the clan."

At midnight, as a full moon lit the campsite, Wolf, the shaman, emerged from his tent and cried out in the wilderness, "We are wild men! We must drum!"

"What's this?" I asked the pudgy wild man named Cougar.

"The shaman is calling for a drum circle," he said. "That's where we sit around and pound out ancient manly rhythms."

"Can I join in?" I ask.

"I suppose so," said Cougar, "but it's bring-your-own-drum, and where are you going to find a drum in the woods?"

Lost as I was in the blinding fog of amnesia, I didn't have a clue. But still, some muted intuition told me I was not the kind of guy to travel far without percussion. So I followed a murky hunch, which led me to the ditch-bound El Camino, where I found a duffel bag stuffed with a baffling array of accessories—a lava lamp, a mini espresso machine, a framed photo of Louis Prima, and a spare set of L'eggs, go figure. I had to dig all the way to the bottom to find what I was after.

When I got back to the campsite, the drum circle had already formed, and I was impressed by the variety and originality of the percussion instruments my wild friends brandished. One guy had a bowl-shaped African tribal drum made from the bristly hide of a bushpig. Another had a deerskin war drum of the Iroquois tribe. I spotted a big flat Celtic drum, a ceremonial wedding drum from Borneo, a kettle-shaped rowing drum from a Polynesian outrigger, and a Laplander drum made from the gleaming pelt of a seal. I was the only guy with bongos.

The shaman was at the head of the circle. "Remember as we drum," he said, "that our goal is to connect our souls, spirits, and bodies with the ancient healing rhythms of times and peoples past. Open yourself up to the joy and power of the primal rhythms," he said. "Let the wild man inside you rise."

Then we started drumming, and I guess my wild man isn't the shy type because in a couple of minutes I had whipped myself into a frenzy of primordial percussion. Novas where exploding in my brain. Mountains were crumbling. Volcanoes were raging and rivers of lava poured white-hot through my being. With transcendent, syncopated gusto, I beat it all out on the bongos.

What I think was happening, see, was that I had tapped into the collective unconscious of all my handy ancestors. I saw Paleolithic Vinnie, surrounded by mocking clan mates, as he bowed over his cave fire to chip the world's first hand tools from stone. I saw Aboriginal Vinnie, shrugging off the pleadings of concerned fellow tribesmen, insisting that his boomerang dream really would come true. I saw ancient Inuit Vinnie trying to convince his shivering neighbors that you could be so warm living in a house made out of ice. And I saw diminutive Pygmy Vinnie whittling away creation's first blow-dart gun, the crafty invention that would finally earn him some respect out on the Serengeti, and get those lanky, wiseass Zulus to knock off singing that condescending "Short People" song once and for all.

Then the visions changed: I saw myself surrounded by a mob of leering little elfish creatures; I saw a giant cartoon chicken squatting on my house; then I was smacking my thumb with a hammer; then my head was stuck behind a toilet; then I was toppling headlong from a roof. . . .

It was a riptide of riveting images, all of them searingly authentic. Even in my drum-induced trance, I knew it could mean just one thing:

"My name is Vinnie! And I . . . am handy!"

Then my memory returned with a gush of primal joy, which expressed itself to me as an ancient, familiar rhythm throbbing in my veins. Unconsciously, I copied that beat as loud as I could on my bongos.

Then there was shouting. Somebody shook me.

Someone was trying to wrestle my bongos away. When I came around, I saw all the wild men standing above me. They were all flushed and huffy. Some were shaking their spears.

Wolf, the shaman, stepped forward. "Stranger," he said. "I'm afraid you'll have to leave."

"But why?" I pleaded. "I was only beating out the joy and power of the primal rhythms."

"No," he said, with an icy stare. "*We* were beating out the primal rhythms. You were beating out the drum solo from 'Wipeout.'"

I glanced around at the wild men. "You mean, I wasn't in touch with the rhythms of the ages?"

"You were in touch," said Cougar, "with the rhythms of the Fabulous Safaris."

I managed an amiable smile. "Hey," I said, "wanna try my bongos? Interesting story here. My uncle Ninootz—a well-known Greenwich Village handyman back in the fifties—bought them from a struggling young writer named Jack Kerouac. Paid five bucks for them. Kerouac wanted ten, but my uncle told him to hit the road. Heh. Heh-heh."

Then the unamused wild men led me away at spear-point and helped me push the El Camino from the ditch. The car was battered but road worthy, and in no time, I was motoring out of the woods and back to civilization.

25
Beef Jerky

I drove all night and arrived home late the next morning, still smarting from the cruel rejection of my woodsy brothers. Someday, I vowed, I'd go back to the woods and prove to them that I am every bit as wild and butchy as the next guy, but for now, all I could think of was a long, soothing soak in a hot bubble bath. When I stepped through the door, I found Angie hanging strips of meat on a clothesline she'd strung across the living room.

"Some new Mongolian delicacy?" I asked, worried yet hopeful.

"I'm making beef jerky," she snarled. "I figure, if you're not going to do something about our dry air problem, I might as well make the best of it."

Crimeny, I grumbled, everything is theater with this

woman. But she did have a point. In the winter months, living in our comfy little bungalow feels like being trapped inside one of those Popeil miracle food dehydrators. You know the feeling, I'm sure. You get raspy in your throat and nasal passages. Your skin flakes and itches. Your joints creak. Your eyeballs scrape in their sockets. Even your dog suffers, for when the water evaporates from his bowl, he is seized, like a thirst-crazed desert straggler, by the shimmering illusion of a deep pool of sparkling blue water, swirling, irresistibly, on crystal white shores. (Well, hey, something makes him drink from the john.)

Unless you're an ancient Egyptian priest and you need to freeze-dry a pharaoh or two, this life-sapping aridness just doesn't have an upside. So, after Angie's gentle prodding, I decided to bone up on the ins and outs of residential humidity, and see if I could make our cozy crib a little less Gobi-like this year. And right away I discovered something surprising.

According to the experts, most families produce enough household humidity from routine household chores, like showering, cooking, and doing the dishes, to keep their homes comfortably humid even in the driest depths of January. The problem, see, is that in wintertime, the bone-dry air outside is constantly trying to suck moisture out of your house, through leaky windows, loose doors, and uninsulated walls.

That's why dryness is usually not a problem for people in tight, new, energy-efficient homes. Good for them; they'll save bundles on Lubriderm. But what about those of us who live in dry and drafty old houses?

Well, first, you get your hands on a hygrometer, which is a gadget used to measure relative humidity. (There are lots of brands on the market, and the cheaper models are generally useless, so spend a little more and make sure you get one that works.)

Now, follow the directions for your hygrometer and read your home's relative humidity. Some experts call for indoor humidity levels of thirty or forty percent, but research shows that most people are comfortable with a level as low as twenty percent. Anything lower than that and your eyelids start to feel like Pringles.

So, let's say your hygrometer reading puts you at fifteen percent humidity. You're in luck. You should be able to solve your dryness problem by tightening up your house a little. Weather-strip your doors and windows, seal up any leaks, damper your fireplace, add some insulation if you can. The point is to keep most of that free, juicy moisture, generated by everyday living, from flowing outside.

Sorry to say, I wasn't so lucky. Our house clocked in at a desiccating seven percent humidity. I mean, you could cure a ham. So my choices were obvious: (1.) pump some moisture into the place damn quick; or (2.) slap up some knotty pine, crank the furnace, and invite the guys from the health club over for a nice, friendly schvitz.

Obviously, I had no choice but to install a humidifier.

If you decide to do the same, there are a few decisions you need to make along the way. First, select a brand certified by the prestigious Humidifier Institute. (That's a real entity, by the way, where earnest researchers in crisp white jackets are laboring selflessly, as we speak, in a tireless quest to better world moisture.)

Next, decide where you want to put it. If you have forced-air heat and a fairly large house, you'll probably want to connect the unit to a warm-air duct, where it will dump a steady stream of moisture into the heated air flowing through all your rooms. This setup requires some minor alterations to your ductwork, a water supply line, and some electrical connections, but it will provide an even distribution of moisture throughout the house.

The alternative is to buy a freestanding humidifier, plug it in, and bask in sudden, whole-house moistness. These independent units work best if placed in a central location, like a hallway or main room, where they can send thin mists of humidity rolling like an invisible fog through your home. No ductwork or blowers are required—the humidity will spread naturally—but you'll need to leave doors open to the rooms you want to benefit. If you don't mind filling the thing with water when needed, you can even skip the water supply line.

Be advised that a freestanding humidifier will not make a gracious addition to your home's decor. So, if you don't like the idea of your guests being greeted by a dorky metal box, shove the thing in a closet. Just make sure there's a register allowing moist air to flow out into the room. Or, you can stash the unit in the basement, with a short run of ductwork leading to a register upstairs.

Next decision: How much moisture output do you need? The sages at the Humidifier Institute recommend one gallon of moisture per day for each room of your house. Resist the urge to overdo it. Excess moisture can cause real problems, especially in older homes without vapor barriers (which are plastic sheets stapled over the studs to keep moisture from migrating outside). For example, dampness seeping through your interior walls could saturate and ruin the wall's insulation or do damage to your home's structural framing. It can even push on out through the outer wall and blister the paint on the exterior siding of your house.

You can't install a plastic vapor barrier in an existing house without ripping down plaster or drywall, but you can provide yourself with a pretty good alternative by giving your interior walls a couple of coats of oil-based semigloss paint.

In any case, make sure your humidifier is equipped with a humidistat, which will automatically regulate the machine's humidity output. Find the lowest setting at which you're comfortable, and forget about it. Ange, by the way, is very happy with our new humidified homestead. She says she sleeps better, breathes easier, feels younger, more supple, more alive. In fact the new atmosphere seems to have affected her in ways I am struggling to understand. Like the other night she comes down the stairs wearing a negligee, she bats her big brown eyes at me, she rubs her hands all over her bare shoulders. "Oh," she says, "doesn't this . . . humidity . . . make you all dreamy?"

I said, "Yeah, dreamy," and offered her some Cheetos.

She sat down beside me and cooed, "I mean, doesn't it whet your appetites?"

I though it over. "Yeah," I said. "As a matter of fact it does."

"Are you thinking what I'm thinking?" She smiled.

"I think so," I replied.

"Exactly what are you thinking?" she purred.

"I'm thinking, I hope there's some of that beef jerky left."

Then she dumped the Cheetos in my lap, stormed up the stairs, and locked herself in the bedroom. I called after her, "Hey, Babe, you brought it up." Go figure. Maybe there's some murky link between humidity and mood swings that science has yet to comprehend. I think I'll call the boys over at the Humidity Institute, see if they'll send out a field team.

26
Vinnie's Inferno

Dear Nick,

Even though I don't know where you are, I am writing this letter to tell you that I miss our sessions very much, and am sorry I reduced your house to rubble. I wish you were here now, because there are so many things that need sorting out. I'm tired of the handy charade I've been pulling on Angie, but without you to help me find the words, I don't have the guts to tell her the truth. Also, my frustrated how-to urges are backing up on me, like sludge in a silted-up sump pump, and you know that can't be good. I am filled with guilt, regret, and agitation. My Cheetos consumption is in the red zone. I'm getting that stress-related rash again, and I think something's churning down on the unconscious level, because lately I've been dreaming dreams that would curl the hair of an opium fiend.

Last night's nightmare was a perfect example. In the dream, I found myself wandering in a grim, barren landscape of dead twisted trees and steaming rocky crags. Piles of brimstone smoldered all around me. Pools of molten lava bubbled at my feet. But worst of all was the staggering sense of evil that seemed to ooze from the very earth at my feet—the rank moral emptiness; the utter depravity; the pure, horrifying unrepentant absence of handiness.

I looked around. Straight ahead was a huge wrought-iron gate with an overhead sign that read ABANDON ALL HOPE, YE WHO ENTER HERE! A smaller sign beneath it said:

No Soliciting.
All Soul-Related Contracts Final.
"Hell" is a registered trademark of Microsoft, Inc.

In a flash, I knew just what was shaking. Like Dante and Orpheus before me, I'd been whisked into the very depths of the Underworld. Crimeny, I told myself, this is really huge. There must be some spiritual lesson the fates want me to learn; some insight into the nature of good and evil that could change the destiny of mankind and save maybe a million souls. Emboldened now by a sense of mission, I gathered my nerve, fired off a quick Hail Mary, and walked right into Perdition.

Immediately, I found myself in a sprawling chamber where teams of cackling demons inflicted hellish torments upon a legion of helpless doomed souls. Some poor saps were being grilled like prawns in giant cast-iron skillets; others were being stretched on creaking medieval racks; while others still had been strapped to sweaty Naugahyde recliners and forced to watch *Joanie Loves Chachi* reruns on Nick at Nite.

Fleeing from those horrors, I found myself wandering down a long, gloomy corridor lined with forbidding stone archways which, I intuitively understood, were the entry portals to all the specific subdivisions of hell. First, I passed the Lunatic Dictator Annex. Next door was the Phony Televangelist Wing. Other doorways were dedicated to Junk Bond Traders, Militia Kooks, Unrepentant Furriers, Telephone Solicitors Who Call During *Bowling for Dollars,* and People Who End All Their Sentences in a Question?

I don't know how long I stumbled along that corridor, but I must have passed a hundred archways before I came upon the doorway that I recognized as my destiny. My spine tingled as I read the sign above the arch. It read, simply, WAYWARD HANDYMEN, ENTER HERE.

I wanted to turn back and find my way home, but I knew I could not. Powerful forces had brought me here, so I steeled myself and entered Handy Hades.

Inside, a group of dazed do-it-yourselfers, fresh to the afterlife, huddled at the registration desk, while in all the surrounding chambers ghastly tortures were noisily in progress. I heard agonized screams from The Hall of

Really Big Splinters, and muffled yelps from The Room Where Heavy Things Fall on Your Toe. And in the main room, which was visible through a big observation window, I saw a few hundred handymen floundering in a pond of boiling tar. The pond was at the bottom of a rocky crater, and the only way out was a single rickety wooden ladder propped against the crater's steep rock walls. But all the bottom rungs were broken.

"What's this all about?" I asked a nearby demon.

"The guys in the pond are handymen who didn't finish jobs," he said. "Now they're paying for their handy sins."

A demon in overalls strolled over to the edge of the pit. "Please," howled one of the tormented handymen, "fix the ladder so we can climb out of this scalding muck!"

The handy demon shrugged apologetically. "Hoped to get to it today," he said, "but we're swamped. What can I tell you, eternity's our busy season."

"But when can you fix it?" another handyman implored.

"Lemme see," mumbled the demon as he flipped the papers on his clipboard, "how's about I pencil you in for . . . never?"

I felt myself being overwhelmed by horror. Those men in the boiling tar may have been sinners, but they were also my handy brothers. I mean, there but for the grace of God, go I. . . .

Then I began to imagine the types of torments the perversely creative demons of Handy Hades might someday arrange for me, and it was too much to handle. Before I knew what I was doing, I bolted out of there like a Clydesdale with a bottle rocket up his butt.

Demons went flying left and right as I barreled my way out of Handy Hades. I sprinted past the entryway for Artists Who Got Rich Making Paintings That Are Nothing But Simple Sentences Spelled Out in Big Block Letters and veered left at Disgruntled Postal Worker Plaza. It was there that I bumped right into him. He was ten feet tall, with obscenely bulging muscles; huge, rustling bat wings; and the cold golden eyes of a rattlesnake. He was munching a Slim Jim and sneering down at me like a mantis eyeing a cricket.

"Wh-who are you?" I stammered, though I had a pretty good notion.

"I'm Satan," he cracked nonchalantly. "Heard of me?" Funny, I expected him to have the voice of a roaring tiger. Instead, he sounded whiny and feisty all at once, like an infernal Charles Grodin.

"What's your name?" he demanded.

"Vincent Agita," I croaked, stopping myself one millionth of an inch short of curtseying.

"The handyman, right?" said the devil. "Do you know why you're here?"

I nodded soberly. "To understand the torments that await me if I do not mend my handy ways," I contritely mumbled.

"What are you talking about?" said Satan.

"The visions of my spiritual future," I said. "All that

punishment stuff in Handy Hades. Isn't that why you brought me here?"

The devil uttered a derisive snort. "I brought you here because the air-conditioning's on the fritz," he said. "It petered out last night and now all it does is blow out a weak warm breeze. We're hoping you can fix it."

"There's air-conditioning in hell?" I asked.

"We don't use it that much," said Satan. "We've got a pretty dry heat down here. But once in a while it comes in handy."

He led me to a utility room off the corridor. "Air conditioner's in there," he said. "How long will this crap take, anyway?"

"Shouldn't take long," I replied, and I got to work.

So that you may avoid the hell of having your air conditioner conk out on the hottest, sweatiest day of the year, here are my humble trouble-shooting tips. There are two main causes for an air conditioner to lose its cooling capacity—leaks and dirt. Leaks drain the system of refrigerant, and you need a pro to find them, fix them, and recharge the lines.

On the other hand, resolving dirt-related break-downs requires only some simple maintenance any home owner can perform.

For example, a clogged furnace filter, which you can replace for a couple of bucks, can jam the entire air-conditioning system, and choke off the flow of cooling air. Check the filter once a month (it slips into slots in the ductwork just where the big cold-air-return duct joins the furnace—your system manual will show you how to find it) and replace it as often as the manufacturer suggests.

You also need to check your condenser—that noisy metal box with a fan inside that sits out in your yard. The condenser's job is to dissipate the heat your system has drained off from your house. Anything that blocks the flow of air—dead leaves, newspapers, overhanging vines or shrubs—will reduce the condenser's efficiency and make your home harder to cool. So clean, prune, replant, whatever.

Also, don't overlook some common-sense approaches to lighten the load on your cooling system. For example, no air conditioner will function efficiently if your home lacks insulation, or you let hot sunlight stream in through unshaded windows, Likewise, you shouldn't shut your system down at night hoping to save some energy dollars. You're better off keeping the thermostat at a comfortable setting during the day, then knocking it down a few degrees when evening arrives. Filling your house with cool air at night, then keeping your shades drawn in the steamy daytime, dramatically cuts the strain on your cooling system and makes for more comfortable temperatures around the clock.

This is all simple stuff, but just to be on the safe side, have your system professionally checked, cleaned, and adjusted every year, since internal grunge, worn parts, and electrical glitches account for a lot of air-conditioning woes.

"Well, I think we found the problem," I said, pointing to a steaming chunk of brimstone trapped in the blower. "No wonder it's so stuffy in here."

I called a demon over and had him fish out the brimstone with his pitchfork. Almost immediately, the blower turned freely and the room temperature began to fall.

"All fixed?" asked Satan.

"Good as new," I said. "So I guess I'll just be heading home."

"Actually," said the devil, "I need you to stick around just a little bit longer."

"How much longer?" I inquired.

"Let's see," he said, glancing at his wristwatch, "it's two-thirty now and I'm thinking, say, maybe . . . forever?"

I stared, horrified, into the devil's glowing green snake eyes.

"You promised to let me go," I hissed. "How could you lie like that and still look yourself in the mirror?"

"Jeez, I don't know," Satan said. "Think it has anything to do with the fact I'm the freaking Prince of Darkness?" Then he snapped his fingers and two pudgy demons leapt forward to prod me with their pitchforks, deeper into the bowels of hell. They bum-rushed me down through a maze of descending caves and corridors, and did not stop until we stood before a pair of towering steel doors.

"Welcome to the Factory of Evil," said Satan as the

big doors slowly swung wide. "Got a little project going I think might be of interest." Then we stepped inside and into a realm of pure diabolical pandemonium. Fiery explosions erupted all around me; sudden blasts of steam shot hundreds of feet into the sky; and the rocks beneath my feet quivered with the hellish rumble of a thousand infernal machines.

As my eyes adjusted to the darkness, I saw a sight that chilled me to the bone: a Satanic maze of conveyor belts zigzagged through the darkness and off into infinity, and rumbling along on those belts, with looks of pure evil glowing in their beady little eyes, was an endless procession of grinning plaster garden gnomes.

"Look at my little darlings," cooed Satan as the parade of hellish trolls toddled by. "Look at their leering little faces. I want you to love them," he said. "I want you to nurture them like a father."

"Please," I said, reeling in horror. "I just want to go home."

"This is your home!" laughed Satan as he led the demons back out the door. "Don't you get it? I'm making you head man on the gnome project. I need six million of these babies by morning." Then he slammed the big steel door behind him. The thundering sound was so lifelike it woke me from my slumber, and I found myself bathed in sweat and tangled in the bedclothes, on the lumpy basement sofa. Ange was coming down the stairs.

"Another nightmare?" she said. "I heard you screaming."

"I had that dream again," I fibbed. "You know, the one where I'm giving Ernest Borgnine a leg waxing."

"You should knock off the Taco Bell binges at bedtime," she said. "And you should tell Nick about that dream. Aren't you due to see him?"

"Overdue, Babe," I replied. "But I plan to see him soon." I meant that, Nick. I'll find you if I have to travel to Handy Hell and back. And then, what a happy little handy devil I shall be.

27
Little Vinnies Everywhere

So the holiday season descended upon the Agita household, and my basement workshop was littered still with the shattered remains of Mrs. Plumpton's nasty plaster garden gnomes—the ones I'd blasted like skeet last spring, when my fiesty new nail gun accidentally burped off a full clip of galvanized framing nails and turned the quiet backyards of our neighborhood into a scene from a Quentin Tarantino movie.

I'd promised Ange I'd have the leering little trolls all patched up and back in service by Christmas Eve, but there were dozens of the little weasels, and by mid-November, I'd managed to fix no more than six. I couldn't help it. I feared them. I just couldn't stand to be near the loathsome little toads. Their eyes follow you. And they're all the time grinning. I mean, what the *hell* is so funny?

"You need to talk this over with Dr. Nick," Ange said one morning. "You can't let your fears stop you from fulfilling your obligations."

"I'll mention it next time," I said.

"Maybe I should come with you," she said. I gave her a quizzical nod, which in Agita-speak can be roughly translated as "Are you referring to *this* particular lifetime?"

"I'm serious," she said. "I saw this story on *Dateline*. They treated phobia patients by exposing them to their fears. Like, a woman who was afraid of heights had to go up to the roof of an office building, and a person who was afraid of snakes had to go to the reptile room at the zoo."

"Sounds cruel," I mentioned.

"It's all done gently," she said, "and under professional guidance. The idea is, by exposing yourself to the object of your phobia, you gradually disarm your fears."

"You want me to expose myself to the gnomes?" I said.

"I want you to confront your fear," she said. "We could bring a gnome to the office. One of the scariest ones. Nick could put you through the paces, and I'd be there for emotional support."

"And what?" I grumbled. "We huddle around a gnome?"

"You have a problem," snapped Angie. "You need to face your fears. You need to fix those freaking gnomes by Christmas. So plan on it—it's going to be you, me, Nick, and the gnomes."

So I took to casing his house again. There were no signs of life at Nick's place, but oh, how the simple sight of the place filled me with yearning for all the handy fun we'd had there. I'd certainly made my mark: All the windows were covered in plywood. My bright blue tarp was still stretched over the hole in his roof. I had scaffolding rigged all along the east side of the house, where I'd punched holes in the siding in my search for water leaks and wood-muching bugs. And the front yard, where I'd dug to run new water lines, was a battlefield of deep, muddy trenches and rolling piles of excavated dirt.

I walked up to the house and pounded on the door. The echo inside was dishearteningly hollow. I checked the mailbox—empty. I stood on my toes and peeked through the door's window, but nothing inside had changed—sheets were draped over furniture; dust bunnies drifted across the hardwood floor.

With a heavy heart I turned to go back to the car and saw Angie standing on the sidewalk. She had a gnome in her arms, and a look of slack-jawed disbelief on her face. She looked a little awestruck, actually, and

VINCE RAUSE

for one lunatic moment, I thought she might just be impressed.

"You followed me," I said.

She ignored me. She couldn't take her eyes off the handy battlefield behind me.

"You did this," she said, dropping the gnome on the lawn. "You ruined Nick's house."

"It's not ruined," I said, stepping away from the fallen plaster troll. "It's becoming reborn."

"When you started with Nick," she said, "I told you not to fix anything."

"It was just a little plaster patch, is all," I explained. "Things sort of mushroomed. . . ."

Then Angie's lower lip began to tremble, which is never a good sign. "He dumped you, didn't he?" she said, grabbing me by the collar. "You actually got dumped by a shrink!"

"I'm thinking of it more as a hiatus," I explained.

"Do you understand what you've done?" said Angie. "This man is a therapist. Every day of his life, he opens his doors to a parade of very troubled people. Psychotics. Schizophrenics. The deluded. The confused. People who think their pets are scheming to get at their bank accounts. People who wear three overcoats at a time. He even does work with the criminally insane. And in all the years he's been in practice, not one of those poor people ever wrecked the house he lives in, and none of them ever got dumped by their shrink!"

"Not to disagree with you, Ange," I said, "but the kind of people you describe shouldn't be handling power tools in any case."

Angie released her grip on my collar and walked back to her car. "You are going to find Dr. Nick," she said. "Then you are going to make this house livable again. I'll be staying at my mother's house. Don't call me until this madness has all been set right."

Then she stomped off to her car, heedless of my desperate exhortations. "Angie!" I cried. "You forgot your gnome."

For weeks, I searched the town for my wayward therapist. I showed his picture in shrink bars and the self-help section at Barnes and Noble. I haunted his favorite coffeeshop. I pumped his friends and patients for leads. But the trail was cold and I was running out of tricks, so, in desperation, I pried a sheet of plywood from one of Nick's missing windows and slipped quietly inside.

I don't know what I was looking for—an address scribbled on a forgotten notepad, a beckoning letter from an old love, anything to help me make sense of Nick's baffling disappearance. But after two hours of fruitless searching, I gave up, and plopped down in the familiar leather swivel chair where I'd passed so many therapeutic hours in pursuit of the troubled handyman within.

"Where are you, Nick?" I said to the darkness. "And why didn't you say good-bye? There are so many questions I wanted to ask you. So many things I wanted to say. . . ."

As I spoke, I let the beam of my flashlight play around the room, and as it swept beneath Nick's chair, it flashed on something shiny—a popped nail head rising out of the hardwood floor. That could mean a loose floorboard, which could mean annoying squeaks. And, oucheewawa, the nasty boo-boo it could wreak upon your bare tootsies.

Naturally I wondered if there were others like it, so I fell to my knees and trained the flashlight on the boards. And that's when I found what I was looking for—a matchbook cover from a lowlife waterfront bar called the Zodiac. Nick wouldn't go to a dive like that. The matchbook must have been dropped by one of the bar's unsavory patrons. For the first time, I feared for Nick's safety. I had to get to the bottom of this. Fortunately, I was in the mood for a little grog.

Just my luck it was karioke night at the Zodiac, so parking was impossible. Also, the signage wasn't very good. And the lot was very poorly laid out. And the moon was *right* in my eyes.

What I'm saying is, I was backing up and I didn't see a thing until I heard the thump. Then I heard a crash, and then a series of crashes, and then a bunch of people shouting.

I got out to reconnoiter. Behind me lay a row of ruined Harley Davidsons that my bumper had toppled like dominoes. As I surveyed the damage, I found myself surrounded by a group of scowling, tattooed men in leather vests and thick-heeled bikers boots, all custom-cobbled, it seemed, for easy, effective stomping.

A guy with a slick-shaved head and wooly mountain-man beard was the first to address me. "You trashed our choppers, man," he said. "You know what that means?"

I grinned nervously and remained silent as a skinny guy with a nose ring and a black, satanic goatee stuck his jaw in my face.

"It means you are so full of anger . . . ," he hissed. The bearded guy nodded. "This kind of lashing out," he said, "it's pointless, and self-destructive."

I surveyed the heap of Harleys. "I'm sure I looked in the rear-view," I said.

"I've seen this so many times," said the skinny guy with the goatee. "He obviously has some unresolved masculinity issues."

The big bearded guy shook his head. "It's projection," he said. "Some resentment against the father."

"Oh please," groaned the goateed guy, "always with the father. Talk about your one-note johnnies. . . ."

The bearded guy glared. "Are you questioning my competence?"

"All I'm saying is, hello, read a journal now and then . . . it isn't always the father."

The bearded guy fumed. "I read as many journals

as you do," he growled. But the goateed guy wouldn't quit.

"Father this, father that, everything's father father father. Just because your dad decided he was a woman trapped in a man's body—"

"That has nothing to do with it," the bearded guy snapped. "I'm perfectly capable of separating my clinical judgment from my personal experiences."

"Sure," laughed the goateed guy, "your father shows up at your bar mitzvah in a blonde wig, with hooters that Anna Nicole Smith would die for, and it doesn't affect you at all."

That pushed the bearded guy over the edge. He smashed his beer bottle on the hood of the El Camino, and holding it by the neck, threatened the goateed guy with the jagged edge.

"You're mine," he muttered, "you little Prozac-pushing pissant."

"Bring it on," said the goateed guy, slipping a switchblade from inside his boot. "But first," he said, "ask yourself, are you really mad at me, or is it just that you're bothered by how good your old man looked in those red-satin spike heels?"

Now the big bearded guy howled in rage, and the rest of the bikers, driven by mindless blood lust, urged the two men on. Violence and rage crackled in the air. Then a soft, commanding voice sounded from the tavern's veranda.

"Put down the bottle," said a man standing in the

shadows. Instantly, all was quiet. I watched the man step into the light. He was dressed in black leather, head to toe. His double-breasted cycle jacket had silver studs on the epaulets and down the sleeves. His skintight pants had zippers up the seams. And on his head was one of those shiny-brimmed cop-style caps sported by the young Marlon Brando in one of my favorite movies, *The Wild One.*

I couldn't believe my eyes. If it weren't for the horn-rimmed specs, I never would have known him.

"Nick," I cried, "it's you!"

"Hello, Vinnie," he said. "I knew sooner or later you'd find me."

I glanced at the motley crew of bikers around me. "You know these guys?" I asked.

"This is my posse," Nick replied.

"You joined a biker gang?" I inquired.

"A very special biker gang," he replied. "We're all renegade analysts."

I gave the guys another look. "Biker shrinks?" I said.

Nick nodded. "We call ourselves The Superego-maniacs," he replied. "We ride, we rumble, then we sort it all out."

All of which immediately explained the tattoo on Nick's right arm: It featured a demonic caricature of Freud, with a rattlesnake tongue flicking from his lips and mesmerizing spirals for eyes. Etched beneath the ghoulish image, in spidery black Gothic characters, was

Nick's chilling new motto: "I'm afraid your time is up now."

I stepped up to Nick as his biker buddies righted their choppers and swept up all the broken glass and bits of chrome.

"I can't tell you how sorry I am about your house," I said. "But I promise, if you come home, I won't rest until the place is shipshape."

Nick slipped a toothpick in his mouth and rolled it between his teeth. "Don't worry about the house, Vinnie," he said. "It doesn't matter anymore."

"But, Doc," I said, "I wrecked your home."

"You did me a favor," he said. "You shocked me out of the boring rut I'd slipped into. You forced me to question everything about my life. If it weren't for you, I'd probably have spent the rest of my life in that swivel chair, listening to people's problems, over and over, and nodding sagely, as if I had a clue."

"But, Nick," I said, "you were good; don't tell me you're giving up on the profession."

"Not giving up," he said. "I'm changing. I want to push the envelope a little, test the boundaries of the discipline. Like a certain iconoclastic handyman I know."

Never before, in a life full of handy glory, had my heart swelled so full with affection, satisfaction, and pride.

"Then what will you do with the house?" I asked, once I was sure I wouldn't start sobbing.

"I gave it to those Jimmy Carter habitat people,"

he said. "They're going to have a worthy family in there by spring."

"Admirable," I said, "but where will you live?"

"At the gang's clubhouse," he said. "We're heading there now; why don't you ride along?"

Moments later, I was straddling the back of Nick's chopper, with my arms wrapped around his waist, as we roared along the waterfront and out of the city to the Superegomaniacs' secluded clubhouse in the woods. It was just a ramshackle farmhouse, with American flags hung as curtains, and greasy chopper parts littered across the lawn.

"Better keep your coat on," said Nick as we all trooped up the porch steps toward the kitchen. "It's a little brisk inside."

Brisk was an understatement. I mean, you could store sides of beef. In the corner was an ancient cast-iron radiator, painted shiny silver. I held my hand to it— several of the chambers felt cool to the touch.

"When was the last time you bled this baby?" I asked.

Nick shrugged. "No offense, Vinnie," said Nick, "but bikers don't bleed radiators. We don't clean out gutters. We don't caulk windows. We don't do anything handy."

I laughed off Nick's shortsighted remark. "Too square for you, huh, Easy Rider?" I said. "Tell you what, to make up for wrecking your bikes, let me tune up your heating system. I can have this place all cozy and toasty in no time."

"I don't think so," said Nick.

"It's a very simple procedure," I promised.

Nick snorted. "Where have I heard that before?" he said.

I shook Nick by his shoulders. "Nick," I told him, "even bikers have to trust."

Just then, a guy with a single gold tooth and a tarantula tattooed on his forehead walked in, carrying the gang's beloved mascot—a monitor lizard the size of a sofa.

"Adler's sick," he said. "He's not moving at all."

I gave the cold-blooded little critter the once-over.

"He's freezing, Nick," I pointed out. "Please, let me help."

Now the rest of the gang had gathered around Adler. Nick glanced at them and saw the deep concern in their eyes.

"Okay," Nick told me, "but no funny stuff. Remember, I'm carrying weapons now."

I nodded happily and asked the crowd to make room while I sized up the situation. It was a pretty straightforward hot-water system: The water gets heated by a boiler down in the basement, then a pump called the circulator sends the water off through supply pipes and into the radiators, from whence "radiates" the warmth.

To radiate efficiently, all the radiator chambers must be filled with heated water. Problems arise when air pockets develop in the chambers and stubbornly refuse to budge. The useless air takes up space needed by the warming water, so naturally, the radiator's efficiency declines.

Fortunately, the fix is simple. First, find the radiator's "supply valve." It's just a short pipe rising from the floor at one end of the radiator, with some kind of big knob on the top. Turn the knob counterclockwise until the valve is wide open. This lets the full amount of hot water flow into the radiator.

Next, go to the end of the radiator opposite the supply valve, and find the "bleeder valve." (It's that little metal nozzle-type affair up near the top.) Take a close look at the bleeder valve. If you see a slot inside the nozzle, you can open and close the valve with a standard screwdriver. If it looks more complicated than that, you'll need a special radiator key. (Ask at any hardware store; they'll know what you mean.)

In either case, position an old coffee mug or saucepan under the bleeder valve, and open the valve until water spurts out. If there's air in the system, you'll get some splattering and huffing. When you get a steady stream of hot water, the radiator has been bled.

It took me less than fifteen minutes to bleed all the radiators at Nick's clubhouse. But since the system had rarely been maintained, I decided to perform a quick but essential inspection. In no time, I spotted a very common problem.

"Look there," I told Nick as I pointed at a tiny pool

of water on the floor beneath a bedroom radiator. "Your supply valve has sprung a leak."

Then I pointed out the big nut just beneath the supply valve's shut-off knob. "If you tighten that nut, the leak might stop," I said. "If it doesn't, you'll probably have to replace the "packing"—that's the stringy stuff that seals the valve. You can buy it at hardware stores. To repack a supply valve, just shut off the valve, then remove the valve's supply handle. (It's fastened by a single screw in the top.) With an adjustable wrench, remove the packing nut (you'll need a second wrench to hold the valve body steady) to reveal the "valve stem." You'll see the crummy old packing wrapped around the stem. Just unwind it, and wrap a string of new packing—clockwise, please—in its place.

Next, I led Nick down to the basement and introduced him to his expansion tank.

"Hot water systems use two types of expansion tanks," I said, rapping on the big metal canister hanging above the boiler. "There's the bladder type, which requires very little attention and can only be serviced by pros, and there's this type, which is called, poetically, a 'plain empty tank.'"

I explained that dangerous pressures can build in the plain empty tank, if left unattended.

"See this little doohickey?" I asked, pointing to a small protuberance on the top of the boiler. "This is the pressure relief valve. It releases water when the tank pressure gets too high, so if you see puddles of water on the floor, check the pressure gauge over here on the boiler. Normal pressure is about twelve psi," I told him. "If you're up around thirty psi, it's time to purge that tank."

And that too, I explained, is simple. First, shut off the isolation valve on the pipe that feeds water into the tank, then open the drain valve and let the tank run empty. (To avoid an indoor flood, run a length of garden hose from the tank drain outlet to a floor drain or a sink.)

Purging a plain empty tank is an essential safety measure, I warned Nick, and should be performed once a year, regardless of pressure levels. And if the valve releases water when the gauge says pressures are normal, the relief valve may be faulty, in which case you should call in the professionals without delay.

"A couple of tips, Doc," I said as we climbed the steps from the basement. "A few drops of oil in the circulator pump can extend the life of your system by decades. Your owner's manual should show you how. And here's a tip for boosting the efficiency of radiators in especially cold rooms: a piece of cardboard wrapped in aluminum foil—shiny side out—set behind the radiator will reflect a lot more heat into the room."

By the time we joined the rest of the gang in the kitchen, the house had warmed up nicely, and Adler was happily munching some leftover arugula.

"Nice work, Vinnie," said Nick. "And you didn't get carried away at all." I nodded glumly. "I only wish Ange was here to see it," I muttered.

"How are things going between you two?" Nick inquired.

I smiled sadly. "Ange left me, Nick," I said. "She's staying at her mother's and I don't think she'll come home until I convince her that my handy urges are completely under control."

"How do you plan to do that?" Nick asked.

"I don't know," I admitted. "I don't know if it's possible."

Nick nodded in understanding. "You're going to have to make a difficult choice here," he said. "It's Angie, or it's your tools. I don't see how you can have it both ways."

I acknowledged Nick's insight with a frown. "Angie's all I live for," I said, "but handyness is what I *am*. How can I stop being me? What would I have to give her?"

Nick shrugged. "It won't be easy," he said. "You have to step out of yourself. You have to stand in Angie's shoes. Force yourself to see things through her eyes, for once. Stop overwhelming her with your own handy needs. Think of her needs, instead."

And just like that, bingo, it clicked. I mean, a guy can be a blockhead all his life, and then someone forces you to face a truth you can't deny, and just like that, badabing! The lights go on. How blind and selfish I'd been, obsessing on my own handy urges while *Angie's* handy needs went unrecognized and undeveloped!

"Come on, Vinnie," said Nick. "I'll drop you off at

your car, but we'll have to hurry. Got a rumble scheduled with a rival gang, the Jung Rebels. Bunch of wussy pseudomystics on Kawasakis."

Then, we rumbled off into the night, Nick toward his two-fisted destiny, and me toward a homecoming that would make or break my hopes of a happy life.

Days later, I was crouched behind the water heater in my dark basement workshop, hoping that the handy fates would smile upon my bold but risky plan to win back the love of the long-absent Angela Agita.

I'd worked on the strategy for days, but now, as I hunkered in the shadows, I wondered: Was this a romantic masterstroke I had hatched, or only a harebrained scheme that would backfire horribly and ruin my life forever? Only time would tell. I was walking the razor's edge here, trusting on instinct alone.

Here's what I had going: Earlier that morning, I'd called Ange at work and left a message on her machine. I told her I'd found Nick and resolved the matter of his ruined house. I also explained that I'd fixed all of Mrs. Plumpton's ghastly garden gnomes, and would deliver them to her by Christmas Eve, as promised. I asked her to come to the house so we could talk. And then I hit her with the closer:

"I know we've been through a lot," I said, "but we need to patch things up and move on, because we're not getting any younger, Babe. And I've been thinking—this may be out of the blue—but we've got lots of room, and lots of love; maybe it's time to add a Little Vinnie to our lives. Or heck, maybe a houseful of Little Vinnies. . . ."

It wasn't something we'd really discussed, but I could tell, by the way Ange was getting all dreamy-eyed anytime we were around some cute little baby, that the alarm on her biological clock was only moments from sounding off. It may have been a smidgen underhanded, to use such an intimate urge as a lure, but I was fighting to save our future here. I had to make sure she would show.

And finally, she did. I heard her key turn in the front door lock, then I heard her footsteps cross the living room floor. She called my name softly, then came down the basement stairs. Immediately, she spotted the solitary gnome I'd placed in the center of the workshop, with a single spotlight trained dramatically upon him, and his back turned toward the stairs. Just as I'd hoped, she approached the gnome and spun him around by the shoulders.

As I'd promised, the once-damaged gnome was whole again, and looking good as new. The glue joints were so tight they were practically invisible, and the high-quality metal-flake auto paint I'd airbrushed on gave the little imp a more colorful and lustrous gleam. I'd made him better than before, and left Mrs. Plumpton nothing to complain about, except, perhaps, for one inspired modification: I'd given the leering little troll a friendlier, more familiar face, molded from a life mask cast of my own rugged yet amiable kisser.

Indeedy: I'd created an alter-gnome; I'd remade him in my own elf-image.

Ange let out a tiny yelp when she realized it was my beaming mug smiling up at her from under the corny Peter Pan cap. Then she tugged away the canvas tarp with which I'd covered the rest of the gnome congregation. When all the gnomes were uncovered, Ange fell speechless, for there, before her, stood row upon row of my sawed-off plaster look-alikes—a veritable grinning throng of little elfish me's.

As reality sank in, Angie's face darkened like a thundercloud. "A roomful of little Vinnies," she hissed. "He's finally gone insane."

The moment of truth had arrived. Angie's rage was spiraling toward eruption, but how would she react? Would she turn around and storm out of my life forever? Or would she notice the sledgehammer leaning against the work bench, so innocent yet so tantalizingly within her reach?

The hammer was the new Lady Vandal six pounder, with a hot-pink nylon handle and softly cushioned neoprene grip. Sleek and colorful as it was, it would not be hard to notice. But it was all up to Angela now. I'd done everything I could do.

The seconds hung like hours as Angie contemplated how she would vent her fury. Her dark eyes darted menacingly back and forth, and they flashed when her gaze fell upon the Lady Vandal.

For an eternity, Ange brooded upon her choices.

Then she reached out slowly. Deliberately, she wrapped her slender fingers around the hammer's stylishly tapered shaft. And as she drew the sledge to her, she smiled down savagely at the nearest grinning gnome.

"C'mere, Little Vinnie," she whispered. "I have a message for your old man. . . ."

Her first few swings struck only glancing blows, chipping off an ear here, the tip of a nose over there. But as she adjusted her stance and her grip, she fell into a brutal rhythm, and the workshop soon became a killing field for the hapless gnomes. At first, she was methodical—she'd use a golf swing to knock the plaster heads off the bodies, then chase the rolling noggins across the workshop floor, like some murderous game of croquet. When the heads stopped rolling, she'd pounce upon them, using an overhand stroke to pulverize each one into dust.

But as she worked her lather up, she surrendered to more wanton destruction. She bludgeoned wildly, randomly, grunting and gasping with malicious intent, as she rained down doom upon my little plaster lookalikes, gradually reducing them all to sad, scattered piles of gnome-rubble.

How long the mayhem lasted, I can't say. I just buried my head as plaster shrapnel filled the air and my wife descended into someplace dark and primal and handy.

Finally, all was quiet. When I stepped out from my hiding place, Ange was slumped back against the

Maytag, with the battle-scarred hammer lying across her lap. Her hair hung loose and wild, her nylons were in tatters, her breathing was rapid and ragged, and her eyes were focused far away. It took her a good thirty seconds to realize I was standing before her. Her voice was soft and husky when she spoke.

"Oh, Vinnie," she whispered, "I never would have *dreamed . . .*"

Gentlemanly honor forbids me from sharing with you the explicit details of the long passionate hours that immediately ensued. (But if you saw the movie *Ghost,* and thought the scene at the potter's wheel was hot, let me remind you that Ange and I were expressing our bottomless love in a fully stocked handyman's work- shop. See what I'm saying?—bungee cords, power buffers, big sloppy tubs of drywall mud. For the true handy romantics among you, no more need be said.)

And since that golden day when Ange connected with the transforming power of her handy soul, our life together has been one unbroken circle of love and tools. Now we tear down walls together; we spend long, inti- mate hours, arm in arm, browsing the shelves at Home Depot and Builder's Square. And just this spring, we built a three-story bamboo tree house in the towering oak behind the house, complete with sunporch, solar- powered paddle fans, and a system of sturdy vines for easy Tarzan-style swinging.

All of that was Angie's idea, which just goes to

show what I've always insisted: In every passionate spirit, handy urges dwell. Sure, they may be stifled by convention, or buried under layers of denial. But once they are coaxed to the surface—once you taste the heady brew of Handiness Unbound—there's no going back to the tamer, grayer world of the prudent and the nonhandy.

Plus, once you're in spiritual synch with your inner handy self, good things seem to happen. For example, out of that memorable afternoon of wanton gnome-smashing and the searing handy passion that followed, came the greatest gift of all—a beautiful son, Vincent Agita Jr., who will not sleep without his big plastic baby tools at his side, and whose rather large and hairy baby noggin is constantly getting wedged in various tight spaces. Ange finds it upsetting, since it happens so often, but to me it means the kid is not going to let a few minor bruises, or a set of chafed and swollen ears, deter his urge to explore.

By the way, if you don't have kids, forget all that nonsense about babies killing the romance in a marriage. You have to work at it, is all; you have to make time for *l'amour.* For example, last Friday was our tenth anniversary. Ange sent Little Vinnie off to sleep at Grandma's house, and when I got home I found her beckoning from the top of the stairs, wearing only a fetching smile and the new rawhide tool belt I'd bought her for her birthday.

As I stood transfixed, Angie drew the cordless drill from its holster, and revved it in the air.

"What do you say, Cowboy?" she drawled. "Wanna get handy?"

So, do you see what I'm saying? When you don't let society define you, when you aren't afraid to follow your bliss, when you refuse to be intimidated by federal regulations and product warning labels, and when cranial hematomas become for you a sign of emotional growth, then life becomes one happy, sprawling construction site, and handiness becomes its own reward. So don't just sit there waiting for your life to happen. Go out and fix something, Bub!